THE

MONTICELLO COOK BOOK

THIRD EDITION

REVISED

THE UNIVERSITY OF VIRGINIA
HOSPITAL CIRCLE

THE DIETZ PRESS, INC., *Publishers*
RICHMOND, VIRGINIA

Printed in the United States of America.

ISBN 0-87517-005-6

Acknowledgments

The Third Edition of the MONTICELLO COOK BOOK represents the interest and labor of many.

Acknowledgment is tendered Mrs. James Taylor Robertson, Food Editor of the *Richmond Times-Dispatch*, for the inspiration given by her article, "Cooking and Eating in Virginia", published in the University of Virginia *News Letter* of April 1, 1949.

Acknowledgment is gratefully made to Mrs. Henry B. Mulholland for her kindly interest in this edition of the MONTICELLO COOK BOOK, and for her coöperation in connection with the copyright.

To Mr. W. Allan Perkins, attorney at law, expression is made of our sincere appreciation for his unfailing courtesy, the generous use of his time, and his invaluable advice in connection with the legal problems involved in the publication of this volume.

The University of Virginia Hospital Circle hereby makes acknowledgment of its lasting indebtedness to Miss Helen Cunningham, who, as Chairman of the Monticello Cook Book Committee, gave unstintingly of her time and energies in the preparation of the manuscript.

Special acknowledgment is made to Mrs. George B. Zehmer, Mrs. Armistead C. Gordon, Jr., and Mrs. Frank A. Geldard, through whose untiring efforts the recipes for this edition of the Cook Book were collected, reviewed, and approved.

Thanks are also rendered Mrs. Charles Henderson, Mrs. Heman J. Redfield, Jr., Mrs. Alfred P. Kehlenbeck,

ACKNOWLEDGMENTS—*Continued.*

Mrs. James E. Kindred, and Mrs. Richard H. Henneman for their advice and assistance.

Sincere thanks are given to Mrs. Oron J. Hale, President of the University of Virginia Hospital Circle, whose continued interest and coöperation have been an important factor in the achievement of our goal.

Appreciation is hereby expressed to Mrs. Atcheson L. Hench and Mrs. Joseph L. Vaughan, who, as members of the Committee on Business and Finance, have, through their consideration, judgment, experience, and advice, contributed materially to the confidence of the Hospital Circle in the success of this venture.

Deep appreciation is tendered Mrs. Edwin M. Betts for her interesting sketches of Jefferson's "Monticello", used to illustrate this book.

Grateful acknowledgment is made to the many members of the University of Virginia Hospital Circle and the community who so generously contributed their favorite recipes, and thus made this edition of the Cook Book possible. Their names are given below.

Mrs. Edwin A. Alderman
Mrs. Vincent W. Archer
Mrs. William E. Atkinson
Mrs. George Austen
Mrs. Franklin Bacon
Mrs. Paul B. Barringer
Mrs. George Barton (*Lexington Cook Book*)
Mrs. Elizabeth W. Beauchamp
Mrs. Virginia Carver Beck
Mrs. Edwin M. Betts
Mrs. Francis Stanton Blake

ACKNOWLEDGMENTS—*Continued.*

Blue Ridge Club
Mrs. Anna Bocock
Mrs. Murray Boocock
Mrs. Anna Bowcock
Mrs. Gordon M. Buck
Mrs. Helen Duprey Bullock
Mrs. Edwin Burton
Canteen Cookery
Mrs. George W. Case
Mrs. Jacquelin Caskie
Mrs. Bruce Chalfin, Jr. (Plantation Gardens
  Herb Farm)
Mr. Bernard P. Chamberlain
Mrs. J. Albert Cheape
Mrs. Nelson Cheney
Christ Church Sewing Society
Mrs. Harry Clemons
Miss Louise Cocke
Mrs. J. A. Cole
Mrs. Thomas Bolling Coles
Mrs. Robert F. Compton
Cordon Bleu
Mrs. Colgate W. Darden, Jr.
Mrs. Herbert A. Donovan
Miss Annie Douglas
Mrs. Alice Gregory Duvall
Mrs. Walter Elcock (*Lexington Cook Book*)
Mrs. Thomas Fawcus
Mrs. George O. Ferguson, Jr.
Mrs. Esther C. M. Fishburne
Mrs. Thomas Fitz-Hugh
Mrs. Richard R. Fletcher

Mrs. James Carroll Flippin
Mrs. Douglas Forsyth
Mrs. Julio Suarez-Galban
Mrs. William Garth
Mrs. Frank A. Geldard
Mrs. Robert Fisher Gibson
Mrs. Charles Glasgow (*Lexington Cook Book*)
Miss Meta Glass
Mrs. Gerrard Glenn
Miss Nancy B. Gordon
Mrs. Robertson Gordon
Mrs. Raymond D. Gorges
Mrs. J. Sharshall Grasty
Mrs. Oron J. Hale
Mrs. W. Ogden Harrison
Mrs. Atcheson L. Hench
Mrs. Charles Henderson
Hotel Chamberlin
Mrs. George Houghton
Mrs. John B. Huffard
Mrs. Raymond Hunt
Miss L. Tabb Huyett
Mrs. Charles Irving
Mrs. Harvey E. Jordan
Mrs. E. Runk Kayan
Mrs. Charles W. Kent
Mrs. Delos Kidder
Mrs. Fiske Kimball
Mrs. Matthew Lawman
Mrs. Ivey F. Lewis
Lexington Cook Book
Mrs. J. Gordon Lindsay
Mrs. James H. Lindsay
Mrs. Arthur H. Lloyd

ACKNOWLEDGMENTS—*Continued.*

Miss Julia Logan
Miss Martha McCleery
Mrs. E. O. McCue
Mrs. Francis H. McKnight
Mrs. John McLean
Mrs. Ashton McMurdo
Mrs. A. F. MacConochie
Mrs. Noble T. Macfarlane
Mrs. E. M. Magruder
Mrs. John L. Manahan
Mrs. Linton R. Massey
Mrs. Frank A. Massie
Mrs. John Minor Maury
Mrs. George R. B. Michie
Mrs. Raleigh C. Minor
Mrs. Richmond T. Minor
Mrs. Samuel Alfred Mitchell
Mrs. Stuart Moore (*Lexington Cook Book*)
Mrs. Frederick T. Morse
Mrs. H. G. Moss
Mrs. Henry B. Mulholland
Mrs. John H. Neff
Mrs. Herman D. Newcomb
Mrs. John Lloyd Newcomb
Mrs. Dan Norton
Miss Mildred Nelson Page
Mrs. W. H. Paine
Mrs. Edwin Perkins
Mrs. William J. Phillips
Mrs. Charles S. Pillsbury
Mrs. William McC. Pitts
Mrs. James Pollock
Mrs. Randolph
Miss Margaret Randolph

Mrs. Heman J. Redfield, Jr.
Mrs. Charles A. Rich
Mrs. Ernest Richard
Mrs. Oreste Rinetti
Mrs. Thomas L. Rosser, Jr.
Mrs. Philip H. Ryan
Mrs. William H. Sage
Mrs. Walton Shanklin
Mrs. J. E. Shepherd
Miss Viola Shields
Mrs. Horatio L. Small
Mrs. Dudley C. Smith
Mrs. Francis Harrison Smith
Mrs. James P. C. Southall
Mrs. Carl C. Speidel
Miss Stella Staples
Mrs. Oscar Swineford, Jr.
The Virginia Housewife
Miss Rosalie Thornton
Mrs. Lamar H. Timmons
Mrs. G. Carroll Todd
Mrs. Oscar W. Underwood, Jr.
Mrs. Joseph L. Vaughan
Mrs. Samuel A. Vest
Mrs. Lyttleton Waddell
Mrs. Robert H. Webb
Mr. William S. Weedon
Mrs. Grace Weinberg
Mrs. Allen N. White
Mrs. Landon White
Mrs. William H. White, Jr.
Mrs. James N. Wilhoit
Mrs. Lucy McGee Wilson
Mrs. Robert Wingfield

ACKNOWLEDGMENTS—*Continued.*

Mrs. Edwin Wood
Mrs. Robert H. Wood
Miss Lucretia Woods
Mrs. Fletcher Woodward
Mrs. George B. Young
Mrs. Albert York
Mrs. Raymond D. York
Mrs. George Baskerville Zehmer

GENEVIEVE F. MORSE, *Chairman*

"Retreat"
March 28, 1950

Table of Contents

CONTENTS—*Continued.*

CONTENTS—*Continued.*

xiii

CONTENTS—*Continued.*

CONTENTS—*Continued.*

CONTENTS—*Continued.*

SALADS

SAUCES

HOT DESSERTS

CONTENTS—*Continued.*

COLD DESSERTS

CONTENTS—*Continued.*

CONTENTS—*Continued.*

xix

CONTENTS—*Continued.*

CONTENTS—*Continued.*

WHAT DOES "COOKING" MEAN?

It means the knowledge of Medea, and of Circe, and of Calypso, and of Helen, and of Rebekah, and of the Queen of Sheba. It means the knowledge of all herbs, and fruits, and balms, and spices; and of all that is healing and sweet in fields and groves, and savoury in meats; it means carefulness, and inventiveness, and watchfulness, and willingness, and readiness of appliance; it means the economy of your great-grandmothers, and the science of modern chemists; it means much tasting, and no wasting; it means English thoroughness, and French art, and Arabian hospitality.

—John Ruskin

Foreword

The tradition of fine cooking that distinguishes the
County of Albemarle in Virginia was inaugurated by
one who may well be called its patron saint, Thomas
Jefferson. Before his sojourn in France as American
Minister he had, of course, enjoyed those indigenous and
time-honored dishes such as batter bread, corn pone,
greens and sweet potato pie, which Patrick Henry de-
scribed as "his native vittels". They doubtless continued
to appear at proper intervals on his table at Monticello.
On reaching France, however, he was at once intrigued,
as have thousands of Americans since then been, by its
culinary art. A vast horizon of delectable new flavors—
including the then unknown vanilla—of combinations,
and dishes, appeared before his enchanted eye. No
sooner was he established in a house of his own, than
he sent James, a slave he had brought with him from
Monticello to Paris, to a *traiteur,* or inn keeper, to be
instructed in this new art. Meanwhile he established a
French cook in his own kitchen. He was not unmind-
ful of the opportunity this offered, and in his own hand
wrote down various of her recipes. Thus it has come
about that our first American recipe for ice cream, a
great novelty at that time, for sponge cake, and various
other delicacies, is in the writing of the third President
of the United States.

Since Jefferson's day other forces have worked for
cosmopolitanism in the cookery of Albemarle. Its smil-

ing country has drawn families from all over the United States. They have brought with them their valued recipes from the Far South, from the Middle West, from the Northern States and from the Coast. They have thus enriched the culinary art of this section, and some of their treasures are here presented in this cook book so aptly named for Monticello.

—*Marie Kimball*

Beverages

ICED COFFEE

To make one gallon, which serves 32 people:

Take 1½ pounds coffee to 5 quarts water.

Put coffee in bag and put in water. Bring to boil and boil ten to fifteen minutes.

Sweeten to taste, but do not make very sweet.

Add 1 pint double x cream, *not* whipped.

Chill.

When ready to put in bowl to serve, add 2 quarts of vanilla ice cream.

Three gallons, or three times this recipe, will serve 100 people.

NOTE: Either coffee or chocolate ice cream instead of vanilla is a good variation.

SPICED TEA

6 bags tea	4 oranges
3 quarts boiling water	4 lemons
½ box cloves	1 cup sugar

Pour 2 quarts boiling water over tea and cloves. Steep. Add sugar. Extract juice from oranges and lemons.

Pour 1 quart boiling water over peel and let stand a few minutes. Add to tea. When cool add juice and strain.

This quantity makes 25 cups.

APPLE TODDY

1 gallon apple brandy **or** whiskey	2 grated nutmegs
1½ gallons hot water, well-sweetened	1 allspice
1 dozen large apples, well-roasted	1 clove
	Pinch of mace

Season with one-half pint good rum. Let stand three or four days before using.

BLACKBERRY WINE

Wash berries, take one quart hot water to one gallon mashed berries. Put in jar to ferment for about three days. The cooler the weather the longer it takes to ferment. Then strain through a thin cloth, one gallon juice, two and one-half pounds sugar. Dissolve well. Put in bottles with thin cloth over mouth to keep insects out. Fill up bottles every day until through fermenting, then cork tightly.   *"Ingleside"*

GRAPE WINE

1½ quarts ripe Concord grapes	2½ pounds granulated sugar

Pick from the stems this amount of grapes and put them in a gallon jug. Cover them with water to within about two inches of the top. After twenty-four hours commence stirring once a day until sugar dissolves. Put loose stopper in jug. After all the sugar has dissolved tie a cloth over mouth of jug and put in a warm place and allow to stand until it has finished fermenting (about a month). Strain through jelly bag and bottle. Wine made in October will be ready for use by Christmas.

"Rugby"

PLUM WINE

There is no recipe for making plum wine, for the creation of any wine is the direction of a natural process, not an arbitrary arrangement of ingredients. To describe this process in twenty words is manifestly beyond the powers of anyone living or dead. Even the taciturn Calvin Coolidge would have shied from such a task. But for those who have plums in abundance, preferably wild goose plums that are reasonably free from internal parasites, the following directions may be helpful.

Mash the plums and let them sit in a large-mouthed container, covered with clean cheese cloth for a day or so to give the busy little ferments a chance; then squeeze the juice through a sack and add the proper amount of sugar. Plums are relatively high in acids and low in sugars, so the quantity of sugar varies from season to season; usually, 1¾ pounds to the gallon is enough. Ferment in an open end barrel or earthenware jar for about ten days, skimming and stirring daily and keeping a clean cheese cloth over the fermenting "vat". Then siphon the young wine into wood or glass containers and close the openings with cotton until the visible signs of fermentation cease. At this point drive in a wooden bung or a cork, seal with paraffin, and forget about the wine until the next spring, when again it may be siphoned off, and this time bottled for ultimate consumption. Owing to its high acid content this wine matures very slowly. Old Plum 1899 is now beginning to be quite good.　　　　　　　　　　　*"Midmont"*

PANTOPS WINE

Mash equal quantities of ripe cherries and blackberries, leave in stone crock for two or three days for fermentation, according to temperature, then strain through cheese cloth. To each gallon of juice add one quart boiling water. Let ferment twenty-four hours, stirring five or six times during the day. Strain again, then add two pounds sugar to each gallon of juice, or more sugar, if desired sweeter.

An yeast cake may be added to this if desired to quicken fermentation. Some vermouth adds greatly to the flavor. Pour in crocks, or gallon bottles, until fermentation ceases, then cork tightly and keep in cool place. A few raisins are an addition to each bottle.

"Credenhill"

EGGNOG

This is the recipe for eggnog which was a favorite in Kentucky and in other Southern States. First estimate the number of persons to be served and measure into a large bowl one punch glass (1 gill) of cream for each person. With this allowance there will be of the finished product about three punch glasses for each person. Then beat the cream stiff in the bowl. In another bowl of approximately the same size as the cream bowl, put the yolks of three eggs for every two of the persons to be served. Beat the yolks stiff in this bowl. Contrary to common belief, the yolks can be beaten stiff, the operation merely requires more time than that of beating the whites. You now have a nearly equal quantity of beaten yolks and beaten cream in separate bowls. Using the punch glass for a measure, pour into a pitcher, or another bowl, for each person estimated, one-half of a glass of rye whiskey, one-fourth of a glass of Jamaica rum, and one-fourth of a glass of brandy, using peach, grape, or French brandy, and dissolve in this mixture one large teaspoonful of sugar for each egg used. The amount of spirits may be varied in either direction according to taste. Now stir the sweetened spirits into the beaten eggs very, very slowly, just as though you were stirring oil into mayonnaise. Then add the whipped cream and stir that in slowly and thoroughly, until the whole mixture has become a perfect blend. Sprinkle a little grated nutmeg on the top of the finished product. Allow the eggnog to stand in a cold place for twelve hours before it is served.   *"Midmont"*

OLD VIRGINIA EGGNOG

12 fresh eggs	1 pint Jamaica rum
2¼ cups granulated sugar	1 gallon heavy cream
1 quart finest brandy	1 cup powdered sugar

Beat the 12 yolks relentlessly, adding the granulated sugar, then alternate shots of the Brandy and Rum till full amounts are incorporated. Then add three-quarters of the heavy cream, and fold in half of the egg whites, pre-beaten in a side dish. Whereupon, beat up other half of egg whites stiffer than stiff, adding to them the cup of powdered sugar, plus (lightly stirred in) the other quart of cream, and fold this sideshow into the main show. Twelve hours' rest in a cool place of safety will be beneficial. Partakers will need spoons, as this calls for spadework. Light sprinkling of grated nutmeg on each cup.   *"Retreat"*

CHRISTMAS RUM PUNCH (HOT)

6 oranges	Whole cloves
½ gallon sweet cider	Ground cinnamon and nutmeg
1 bottle Jamaica rum, bestest	
Sugar to taste	

Stick the oranges full of cloves and bake them in the oven until they soften. Place oranges in the punch bowl,

pour over them the rum and granulated sugar to taste.
Set fire to rum and in a few minutes add the cider slowly
to extinguish the flame. Stir in cinnamon and nutmeg,
and keep the mixture hot.

STRAWBERRY BOWL

The small, wild strawberries which grow near the
edges of plots of wood-land in late spring are very much
to be preferred. Garden-grown or commercially-grown
berries may be used if wild strawberries are unavailable,
but the smaller berries which are fully ripe should, in
this case, be chosen.

Procure a pint and a half of berries and several sprigs
of sweet woodruff. In a bowl or dish which has a flat
bottom, spread a layer of granulated sugar. The amount
of sugar used will vary with the acidity of the berries and
the acidity of the wine. On the sugar, place a third of the
berries and a couple of sprigs of woodruff, and cover
with a layer of sugar. Continue this until the berries
are used up, and there are three layers of the berries
and four of sugar. Cover the bowl, but do not place in
the refrigerator. The preparation of the berries should
take place about six hours before the bowl is made.

Thoroughly chill two bottles of Moselle and one bottle
of dry champagne. Have the punch bowl well chilled.

When you are ready to serve, pour a little of the
Moselle into the dish with the berries and stir gently.
Then slide the whole mixture into the punch bowl. Add
the rest of the Moselle, and stir again. The champagne
should be added after the bowl has been brought before
the company. If the company is small, a piece of ice
may be floated in the bowl. Be sure that each guest gets
a couple of the strawberries in his punch-cup.

Appetizers

CHEESE STRAWS

1 cup grated cheese	½ teaspoon salt
1 cup flour	1 egg (yolk)
½ cup butter	2 teaspoons sweet milk

1 pinch red pepper

Make a dough of ingredients. Cut in strips and bake.

CHEESE WAFERS

1 pound of old sharp cheese	2 teaspoons salt
¼ pound butter	1 teaspoon Worcestershire
1 cup flour	sauce

Dash cayenne pepper

Grate cheese, add other ingredients and mix together until it forms a solid mass. Shape into roll, wrap in wax paper and place in ice box for twenty-four hours. Slice thin and bake eight to ten minutes in hot oven.

"Hollymead"

GARLIC CHEESE ROLL

Mix one pound of American cheese, 2 packages of Philadelphia cream cheese, and one clove of garlic. Roll onto waxed paper sprinkled with paprika and set in a cold place.

COD FISH COCKTAIL BALLS

1 cup shredded cod fish	1 small egg
1 cup mashed potatoes	¼ stick butter
1 teaspoon onion juice	Black pepper

Mix cod fish and potatoes, adding onion juice and egg,

black pepper, and salt if necessary. Make into very small balls and fry in hot fat and spear with toothpicks.

CURRIED SHRIMP CANAPES

Sauté 1 tablespoon of chopped onion in 2 tablespoons of butter. Add 1½ teaspoons of curry powder and 1 teaspoon of chutney. Sauté as many shrimp as you need for canapes in this mixture. Place them on rounds of buttered toast and sprinkle with chopped egg white and parsley.

TOASTED HOT NUTS

Take one cup pecans—stir into sauce made of soft butter seasoned with tabasco, paprika, dash cayenne. Pepper and salt after toasted.

ROQUEFORT PUFFS

Make puff paste as follows:

½ cup butter   1 cup boiling water
3 or 4 eggs   1 cup flour

Bring water and butter to boil. Remove from stove and put in all the flour at once. Replace on stove and stir violently until the paste leaves the sides of the pan, about 1 minute. Chill and put in eggs one at a time, stirring well after the addition of each egg. Drop about 1/3 teaspoon of paste to each puff. Bake in moderate oven about 35 minutes. Make a slit in top of puff and fill with roquefort cheese softened a little with French dressing. Put in hot oven for a few minutes before serving.

These are delicious served with salads, as well as cocktails.

Breads

NOTE: All of the following corn bread recipes are based on the use of white water-ground meal, which is quite different from the usual yellow coarsely ground meal of the West and East. The spoon breads and batterbreads, in particular, would not turn out in the least as intended if made with coarse meal. If you cannot find water-ground meal in your shops, perhaps your grocer would order some for you.

SCALDED BATTER BREAD

1 quart sweet milk
1 cup corn meal
4 eggs

1 teaspoon salt
1 tablespoon butter or
bacon drippings

Put milk in double boiler, save a little to dissolve the meal in when cold. When milk is quite hot add the meal that has already been dissolved in the cold milk, stir until it becomes quite thick, then remove from fire, let cool, then add the eggs that have been beaten with salt, then the butter. Pour into a baking dish that has already been buttered. Bake about 20 minutes and serve as soon as you can.   *"Cloverfields"*

VIRGINIA BATTER BREAD

2 cups of corn meal sifted
3 cups of boiling water
2 cups of sweet milk

1 teaspoon of salt
1 tablespoon of butter
3 eggs

Place butter in baking pan and set on stove to melt.

11

Then put one cup of corn meal in the mixing bowl and pour the boiling water on, stirring vigorously. Add the other cup of corn meal and stir well. Add sweet milk and salt and lastly the eggs well beaten. Stir thoroughly and pour in the melted butter. Then pour the whole mixture into the warm baking pan and bake three-quarters of an hour in a moderately hot oven. If you have a little cold rice left over, one or two tablespoonsful, put in with the meal before the hot water has been poured on; it makes it very nice and is a good way to use the left over rice.

OLD VIRGINIA SPOONBREAD

1 cup white cornmeal	1 teaspoon sugar
3 cups milk, scalded	1 teaspoon salt
1 tablespoon butter, melted	3 eggs

Gradually add cornmeal to milk and cook for 5 minutes, stirring constantly. Cool slightly and add butter, sugar, and salt. Add beaten egg yolks and fold in stiffly beaten egg whites. Bake in greased pan in a moderate oven at 350° F. for about 45 minutes. Serve hot from baking dish with plenty of butter.

As served at The Hotel Chamberlin, Old Point Comfort.

RICE BREAD

1 cup or more of cooked rice	1 teaspoon salt
4 tablespoons corn meal	2 teaspoons baking powder
4 eggs separated	2 tablespoons sugar
1 pint milk	4 tablespoons melted butter

Mix all ingredients folding in last the whites of eggs, beaten stiff. Pour in hot buttered dish and bake 30 minutes at 400° F., or longer at less tempearture.

CORN DODGERS

1 quart white water ground corn meal	1 cup water
	1 teaspoon salt

Sift meal and mix up into dough with cold water and salt. Make up with the hand into long oval shaped cakes and put in a pan to bake. Dot with butter to make a sweet brown crust. These were a daily article of diet of George Washington, father of his country.

VIRGINIA'S CORN MUFFINS

1 cup meal	2 tablespoons *lard,* melted
1 cup boiling water	2 teaspoons baking powder
½ cup milk	1 teaspoon salt
2 eggs	1 tablespoon sugar

Scald meal with boiling water, then add milk. Beat eggs into melted lard, and add to first mixture. Add baking powder, salt, and sugar, and pour batter into greased muffin tins. Bake 20 to 25 minutes in oven of 425° F.

CORN STICKS

1 cup corn meal	¼ cup butter
½ cup hot boiled grits	1 cup milk
¾ cup flour	1 egg
3 teaspoons baking powder	½ teaspoon salt

Sift corn meal, salt, baking powder. Add grits to which has been added butter, milk and well beaten egg. Bake in buttered hot stick pans in moderate oven 20 minutes.

AN OLD FAMILY RECIPE
FOR "LIGHTNING" CORNBREAD

1½ cups meal   ½ cup sugar
½ cup flour   ½ tablespoon salt

Sift all ingredients together and add 2½ to 3 cups boiling water all at once until consistency of very soft mush, that is, until batter looks like cooked cream of wheat for babies. Use pan about size you would use for batterbread. Preheat pan, with about 2 tablespoons bacon grease in it and when hot pour in mixture and bake at 450° F. for 30 minutes.

This is delicious served with a hash and salad.

CRACKLING BREAD

3 cups of meal   Buttermilk, enough to make
1 teaspoon of salt   a stiff batter, which is made
1 teaspoon of soda   into flat cakes with the
¼ cup of shortening   hands and baked in oven.
1 pint of cracklings

FARMINGTON CORN CAKES

3 eggs   1 tablespoon melted butter
1 pint milk   1 tablespoon bacon grease
½ teaspoon salt   Enough *water ground* meal to
1 tablespoon sugar   make a thin batter
1 tablespoon flour   3 teaspoons baking powder

Beat 3 eggs, add milk, add meal, sugar, flour, salt and mix thoroughly. Add shortening and last add baking powder. Stir before each cooking, as meal is inclined to settle at bottom. Griddle should be quite hot. Turn cakes quickly.

BREAD CRUMB CAKES

Soak 1 cup stale bread crumbs in ½ cup of water for 10 minutes.

Add 1 cup milk.

Sift together:

¾ cup flour   4 teaspoons baking powder
½ teaspoon salt

Add 2 beaten eggs and 4 tablespoons melted shortening

Mix well and bake on slightly greased hot griddle.

BUCKWHEAT CAKES

1½ pints Valley buckwheat flour
½ cake Fleischman's yeast
1 egg
¾ teacup of white flour

1 tablespoon of Porto Rican molasses or brown sugar
1 teaspoon of soda
1 teacup of buttermilk

Make batter with lukewarm water. Let stand overnight. In the morning add beaten egg and soda dissolved in the buttermilk.

WAFFLES

2 eggs
2 cups flour
2 cups sour milk
2 tablespoons shortening

1 teaspoon salt
¼ cup meal
1 teaspoon baking powder
1 teaspoon soda

Beat eggs, add milk, flour, meal, salt, baking powder sifted in the flour, soda and shortening.

KENTUCKY BEATEN BISCUIT

6 cups flour before measuring. (A flour milled from soft wheat is much better. In Virginia, Melrose flour is

one. The standard brands such as Gold Medal and Pillsbury are made from hard wheat.)

1½ teaspoons salt	1 cup shortening—Spry or
1½ tablespoons sugar	Crisco

1¾ cups ice water

Sift flour, salt and sugar together. Add shortening
with fingers. Make well in middle and add ice water.
Run dough through the biscuit break (a machine which
does the beating for you) 150 times, working in 1½ cups
of additional flour during the operation. If beating by
hand instead of machine, beat about 30 minutes with
wooden mallet on a block until dough is slick and glossy
and full of blisters.

Roll dough to about 1/3 inch thickness and cut out
with small *glass* cutter or top of small tumbler. Prick
with fork, very deep, as the pricks hold the layers together. Bake 30 to 35 minutes at 400° F. Makes between 5 to 6 dozen biscuits.

CHEESE BISCUITS

1 pound cheese, ground	1 teaspoon salt
2 cups flour, sifted	Red pepper to season

Melted butter

Mix cheese, flour, salt, red pepper, add melted butter
to make a soft dough. Roll, cut in small rounds, bake
in hot oven.

DROP BISCUIT

2 cups flour	1 teaspoon baking powder
½ teaspoon of salt	1 cup cream

Sift together dry ingredients. Add cream. Drop from
a teaspoon on greased pan and bake in quick oven.

CHANEY'S THIN BISCUITS

1 pint flour	2 ounces lard
2 ounces butter	1 saltspoon of salt

Sweet milk to make stiff dough

Make in small balls, roll very thin, stick well, bake a very light brown.

FAT RASCALS

¾ pound butter	1 pound flour

1 pound currants

Mix butter and flour, add enough milk to make the consistency of biscuit dough. Roll out thin, cut into small round biscuits, bake. Split in two and butter. Serve hot. *"Rugby"*

SWEET POTATO BISCUITS

2 cups flour	1 cup cooked mashed sweet
4 teaspoons baking powder	potatoes
1 teaspoon salt	1/3 cup sugar and ½ cup
1 teaspoon grated nutmeg	rich milk or cream added
2 tablespoons Crisco	to sweet potatoes

Sift dry ingredients. Work in shortening. Add the milk and potato mixture which will make a sticky dough. Knead on a floured board. Roll, cut, and prick with fork like biscuits. Bake in hot oven, at 450° F., until light brown.

MADISONS

1½ pounds Irish potatoes	2 quarts flour
2 tablespoons sugar	3 eggs (or 6 yolks)

1 yeast cake (dissolved in ½ cup lukewarm water)

Boil potatoes and mash, add 5 ounces shortening, add

a little flour to cool the potatoes. The dough should be about the consistency of loaf bread. Let rise, drop with spoon far apart in pans. Let rise again and bake.

PERFECT BUTTERSCOTCH ROLLS

2¼ cups milk	½ cup butter or Crisco
2 yeast cakes	2 eggs
¼ cup sugar (heavy)	About 7 cups flour
	2½ teaspoons salt

Scald milk and melt shortening in it as it cools. Mix sugar and yeast until it liquefies. When milk is lukewarm add to yeast and sugar. Add beaten eggs and beat in flour and salt until you have a soft dough. Sprinkle with flour and pat into a ball in the mixing bowl. Cover and set bowl in the ice box until 3 hours before needed.

Generously grease your muffin tins with Crisco or other vegetable shortening. Be sure that you grease them heavily. For every dozen rolls mix 1 cup light brown sugar with ¼ cup butter and put a spoonful in bottom of each section of muffin tin.

Now roll the dough into an oblong shape about ¼ inch thick. Spread with melted butter and sprinkle with cinnamon. Roll in a long roll and cut into pieces about 1 inch thick. Place in muffin tin and let rise in a warm room 2 to 3 hours or until double in bulk. Bake in 400° F. oven about 25 minutes. Be careful that sugar does not burn. Before removing them from oven, have a large flat pan ready and turn the tin over immediately onto this. Lift and let sugar run onto the rolls. Don't burn your fingers.

This recipe can be kept in refrigerator several days and made into rolls as desired.

Oven: 400° F. Time: 25 minutes. Makes: 3 or 4 dozen.

ICE BOX ROLLS

1 cup boiling water	¼ cup sugar
1 tablespoon salt	1 tablespoon butter

Mix together and cool.

Soften 1 yeast cake and ½ teaspoon sugar in a little lukewarm water. 1 egg well beaten.

Sift 2 cups flour, stir in the above liquids and beat well. Add 2 cups flour to form a sticky dough. Place in a greased bowl and cover and place in refrigerator overnight. Let rise 3 hours before baking. Bake in hot oven.

SADIE'S ROLLS

3 Irish potatoes	1 1/3 teaspoons salt
½ cake yeast	1 cup lard
1½ tablespoons sugar	3 pints flour

Mash well cooked potatoes through sieve and let stand in water in which they were cooked until lukewarm. Dissolve yeast and sugar in lukewarm mixture. Thoroughly mix lard and salt in sifted flour. Gradually add potato mixture to flour and lard using more warm water, if needed. Let stand in crock five or six hours, keeping warm but not hot. When well risen pinch off small pieces and pat into shape using melted butter. Put in biscuit pans and keep warm about one and one-half hours before cooking.

QUICK POTATO ROLLS

Six or seven cups of flour   1 cake Fleishman yeast

Boil 4 large potatoes and mash while hot. Stir into this one cup of lard and butter mixed, one tablespoon salt and two well beaten eggs. Into 1 cup milk dissolve yeast cake and 1 tablespoon sugar. Add to potato mixture. Into this stir flour. Set to rise for about 7 hours. Roll out on flour board using just enough flour to handle. Make into rolls. Cover and let rise about 2 hours. Bake about 30 minutes in 400° F. oven.

ENGLISH MUFFINS

1 pint milk	3 cups flour
1 ounce butter	¼ cake yeast
	1 teaspoon salt

Scald milk, add butter, and stand it on one side until lukewarm, then add the yeast, salt and flour. Beat continuously for five minutes. Cover with a towel and let stand in a warm place two hours. When light, add enough flour to make a soft dough, work lightly with hand, divide into small balls. Place each ball in a greased muffin ring and let rise again. Bake on a hot griddle in muffin rings, until a nice brown. When done, break or pull them open as a cold knife makes them heavy. Or split and toast. *"Buena Vista"*

SCOTCH SODA SCONES

1 pound flour	½ teaspoon salt
1 teaspoon cream tartar	1 ounce shortening
½ teaspoon baking soda	2 teaspoons syrup
	Buttermilk

Rub shortening into flour, add all dry ingredients rubbed through sieve. Add syrup and enough buttermilk to make a dough just stiff enough to roll out. Use knife for mixing. Shape into round cakes, just a little smaller than griddle. Divide each cake into 4 and cook each side well on a well-floured heated griddle. *"Cotswold"*

A NEW ORLEANS RECIPE FOR HUCKLEBERRY MUFFINS

4 tablespoons Crisco   2 cups flour
4 tablespoons sugar   1 cup sweet milk
½ teaspoon salt   2 eggs
4 teaspoons baking powder   ½ cup huckleberries

Mix sugar, Crisco and eggs, then add 1½ cups flour, baking powder, and salt, then milk. Do not try to smooth out batter. Dredge the other half cup of flour over berries and add to batter. Bake in hot greased muffin tins.

POTATO FLOUR MUFFINS

½ cup potato flour   ¼ teaspoon salt
1 tablespoon melted butter   3 teaspoons baking powder
1 teaspoon sugar   2 eggs

Mix as for cake and put in warm muffin pans which have been greased. Cook in oven 450° F. for twenty-five or thirty minutes.

POPOVERS

1 pint flour   1 cup milk   3 eggs

Mix flour and milk, and add eggs. Beat vigorously for at least 5 minutes. Pour into hot greased muffin tins. Begin with hot oven, then decrease gradually to moderate oven as popovers begin to brown.

DATE BREAD

1 box dates, chopped   2½ cups flour
1 cup chopped nuts (prefer-   1 cup milk
     ably black walnuts)   2 teaspoons baking powder
3 eggs   1 saltspoon salt or ¼ tea-
1 large cup sugar   spoon

Beat sugar, eggs and salt lightly. Reserve ½ cup flour

Add flour and milk alternately. Then stir in dates and nuts, then add ½ cup flour with the baking powder in it.

Oven: 350° F. Time: 1 hour. Makes one loaf.

NUT BREAD

3½ cups flour	1 cup milk
1 cup sugar (scant)	1 cup nuts, rolled
3½ teaspoons baking powder	1 egg

Sift flour three or four times, mix all well, put in greased pan, let stand 20 minutes, bake one hour.

ORANGE BREAD

Skin of 3 oranges	2½ cups bread flour
1 cup sugar	1 teaspoon salt
½ cup water	3 teaspoons baking powder
1 egg	1 tablespoon shortening
	1 cup milk

Cut fine the skin of the oranges; boil in water until tender. Drain; cook with sugar and water until thick. Cream shortening, add eggs, flour, salt, milk, orange skins, baking powder, and mix well. Let stand twenty minutes. Bake in slow oven for one hour.

SALLY LUNN

When light bread is being made, take 3 cups of risen dough and work into it:

3 well-beaten eggs	1/3 cup of sugar
1/3 cup of butter	A small pinch of soda

When the above ingredients have been *thoroughly* mixed and well-beaten together, put into well-buttered cake pan, or individual molds, and set in a warm place to rise. When twice its bulk, it is ready to bake, and should be eaten *hot*.

SALLY LUNN

1 cup warm milk
½ cup melted butter
2 eggs, beaten very light
1 yeast cake, dissolved in scant ½ cup warm water

1 quart sifted flour
1 teaspoon salt
3 tablespoons sugar

Sift dry ingredients into mixing bowl. Combine milk and butter and add to beaten egg. Make hole in flour and pour in yeast and mix. Then put in the milk mixture.

Beat smooth and set to rise in moderate temperature 3-4 hours. Then stir down and pour into greased tube pan and let rise 2-2½ hours, or until double its bulk. Cover with a little melted butter and bake at 350° F. for 45 minutes or 1 hour.

Soups

MOCK LOBSTER SOUP

1 can Campbell's pea soup   1 soup can of cream
1 can Campbell's tomato   1 soup can of milk
  soup

Four tablespoonsful of cooking sherry, dash of Worcestershire sauce, piece of butter, salt and pepper.

This recipe serves six persons.

Note: 1 can bouillon.

          1 can crabmeat may be added, if desired.

BEAN SOUP

(Soup made from a chicken, turkey or duck carcass and gravy)

To one carcass—of any of the above—use two cups of white or navy-beans soaked several hours in water. Break up the bones, add enough water to cover well; let boil a short time, then add beans and gravy. Boil slowly until beans are soft then strain through a colander, add salt, pepper, Worcestershire sauce, and celery salt.

BLACK BEAN SOUP

1 pint beans   Pepper and salt
6 cloves   ½ onion
              Sliced bacon

Soak beans overnight in three quarts of warm water. Boil in same water with seasonings almost all day.

24

Strain through sieve, add a little browned flour. Serve with slice of lemon, egg, and croutons.

BEEF AND CREAM SOUP

Take 2 pounds of round steak, trim off all the fat, cut in small pieces, cover with cold water and simmer until all juice is extracted.

1 tablespoon of butter
1½ tablespoons of flour

1 cup of milk
½ pint of cream

Put butter in double boiler, add flour, milk and cream, and beef juice. Season to taste and cook until soup is consistency of thick cream. "Very fine."

"Cismont Manor"

BRUNSWICK STEW

3 squirrels, skinned, cut in small pieces
2 pints tomatoes run through colander
1 pint lima beans
1 pint Irish potatoes, cut up fine
½ pound butter

6 ears green corn, cut from cob
½ pound fat salt pork, cut up
1 teaspoon black pepper
½ teaspoon cayenne
1 gallon water
1 scant tablespoon salt

1 onion minced small

Put water on with salt, boil 5 minutes. Put in onions, beans, corn, pork, tomatoes, potatoes and the squirrels, which must have been in cold salted water some time. Cover closely and stew 3 hours very slowly, stirring frequently from bottom. Take off, extract all the bones, cook 1 hour longer, or more, being careful not to burn. Serve hot.

Note: Chicken or rabbit might be used instead of squirrel.

BRUNSWICK STEW

8 to 10 pounds chuck roast   ½ pork shoulder roast (6
3 to 6 pounds hen   pounds)
3 pounds veal

First process. Boil each meat separately, in as little water as possible, until the meat falls from the bones. Shred this meat, pulling it apart with your fingers. Skim all the fat off each kettle of meat before combining the liquids and meats.

Second process. 8 quarts of canned tomatoes, or its equivalent in fresh ones.

5 pounds frozen corn   5 pounds frozen lima beans
                    2 pounds okra

Cook all these vegetables separately in a pressure cooker, or in as little water as possible. Season each one as for the table with plenty of butter, reserving the broths with the vegetables.

Cook 1 gallon of white potatoes and fix as for mashed potatoes, using just butter and salt and pepper for seasoning.

Brown in butter 1 quart finely chopped onion and 1 cup chopped green pepper, and 1 cup chopped celery.

Third process. Combine all ingredients except okra and potatoes in a 30 gallon kettle. Add okra and potatoes towards the last so they won't stick. Simmer, stirring pretty constantly, until all liquids are reduced to the consistency of a thick stew, to be served on a dinner plate. Watch that it does not stick.

Then season with tabasco, Worcestershire, and A-1 sauce, and 1 jar of chili sauce, salt and pepper and sugar to taste.

Quantities are easily reduced, the process being the same, to serve fewer people. This may be made ahead of time and stored in refrigerator for several days. Use tomato juice in small quantity to make liquid to reheat the stew for serving.

Serves: 50.

CLEAR SOUP

1 large can tomatoes	Several cloves
3 cans Campbell's bouillon	2 bay leaves
Salt and pepper to taste	2 or 3 pieces celery
1 green pepper	

Let this simmer slightly 2 or 3 hours, strain and serve hot. Delicious in summer when jellied and served cold.

OKRA OR SUMMER GUMBO

1 chicken or hen	4 dozen okra
1 ham bone or ½ pound salt pork	1 large onion
	1 sweet green pepper
1 pound shrimp	

Cut chicken up and brown in a little hot lard; add okra sliced, onion, pepper and pork cut up, salt and pepper to taste. Cover well with warm water, boil for 2 hours, add shrimp and some corn and tomatoes, if desired. Have a dish of rice to serve with this.

ONION SOUP

One-fourth pound onions, sliced and browned in butter. These are then steeped in 1 quart of consommé. Seasoning is added and the soup is poured into a shallow earthenware bowl. Rounds of French bread are added, cheese is sprinkled over the bread and the soup is then put in the oven to brown.

SOUP—JARDINIÈRE

6 slices bacon cut in strips	2 cups chicken stock
3 sprigs chopped parsley	1 cup grated Parmesan cheese
1 small piece garlic	
1 finely sliced onion	1 cup finely shredded cabbage
2 finely sliced carrots	
2 bunches finely chopped celery	Seasoning

Grind three slices of bacon, garlic and parsley through meat chopper and add to the soup stock. Stir well and add the rest of the bacon, vegetables, and seasoning. Boil slowly in covered pot for one and one-half hours. Serve with grated cheese.

OYSTER STEW

1 quart oysters	5 cups milk
3 tablespoons flour	Salt to taste
⅛ pound butter	Dash red pepper

Bring oysters to boil in stew pan. Heat milk, seasonings and butter in double boiler, saving out enough milk to make a smooth paste with the flour. When milk begins to bubble around edge of pan, pour the cold milk and flour mixture into it, stirring constantly until it thickens. Pour hot milk into the hot oysters, continuing to stir constantly. Return to double boiler and cook over *very* low fire to keep from curdling for 30 minutes. The flavor improves with slow reheating in a double boiler the next day. It must always be kept below the boiling point.

ICED PEA SOUP

Cook well-covered with water until tender the pods from 2 pounds of fresh green garden peas with several slices of onion, 1 stalk of celery, parsley, salt and pepper. Drain. Cook separately the peas and put through a sieve. Add to the first liquid. Thin with cream. Chill well and serve topped with chopped chives.

"Red Fields"

POTATO AND TOMATO SOUP

2 large onions.

Slice them and cook them gently in ¼ cup butter, covering them and stirring once in a while. They must not brown. Add:

2 cans consommé	Salt, thyme, marjoram and
2 cups canned tomatoes	basil

Cook for half an hour. Add:

2 cups sliced potatoes and	3 cups water

Simmer, covered, until potatoes are soft. Rub everything through a sieve, add a bit of cream if you like, and serve with grated Parmesan cheese and croutons.

POTATO SOUP

3 potatoes	Salt to taste
1 quart milk	¼ teaspoon celery
2 slices onion	⅛ teaspoon pepper
2 tablespoons butter	2 bouillon cubes (chicken)
2 tablespoons flour	1 teaspoon dried sweet basil
1 teaspoon finely chopped parsley	

Cook potatoes with onion in boiling salted water. When soft either rub through a strainer or mash fine with potato masher. There should be 2½ cups into which dissolve cubes. Heat milk and add to potato mixture, using a whisk. Melt half the butter, add dry ingredients, and stir until well mixed. It is best to add some of the warm milk to keep it smooth. Boil one minute and add sweet basil and parsley.

LOUISIANA SHRIMP GUMBO

2 quarts fresh okra	Salt and pepper to taste
2 slices cooked ham, cut in cubes	2 chopped onions
	1½ pints raw shrimps
½ pint fresh oysters	2 bay leaves
Sprig thyme	1¾ quarts water

Put okra and onions in frying pan with small amount of lard or cooking oil. Fry slowly, stirring all the time, cook until soft and dark in color. Add water, add seasoning, then shrimps and ham. Add oysters 10 minutes before gumbo is done. Serve with rice. Chicken or fresh crab meat can be substituted.

"Castalia"

Luncheon & Supper Dishes

CHEESE SOUFFLE

4 tablespoons butter	½ teaspoon salt
4 tablespoons flour	⅛ teaspoon dry mustard
2 cups milk	⅛ teaspoon paprika
2 cups grated sharp cheese	⅛ teaspoon soda

3 eggs, separated

Melt fat in sauce pan. Add flour while stirring. When this is smooth, add milk, salt, mustard, paprika and soda. As this mixture thickens, add grated cheese, stirring until smooth again. Pour over beaten egg yolks and when blended, fold in whites, stiffly beaten. Pour into large greased casserole, set in pan of water and bake in moderate oven at 375° F. for 45-50 minutes until firm.

Serves 6.

CHICKEN LIVERS, GIZZARDS, AND HEARTS WITH BACON

Boil 6 sets of giblets for about 15 minutes in boiling, salted water. Drain them and let cool. While waiting put 1 tablespoon chicken fat in frying pan and cut 1 onion very, very fine, and sauté. When giblets are cool enough to handle cut in real fine pieces and sauté with onion. Add 2 teaspoons flour and stir so it is well mixed with fat. Add 1 cup of chicken broth and heat until thick. Serve on toast with a strip of bacon across each serving.

When I buy my giblets, sometimes they are just gizzards, and haven't any chicken fat or broth, I use bacon fat and cream or top milk.

Serves: 4.

CHICKEN RING

2 cups cold chicken, diced	Salt
1 cup scalded milk	Pepper
4 egg yolks	Grating of nutmeg
2 tablespoons lemon juice	(optional)

Beat egg yolks until light and add to hot milk. Add chicken and seasonings. Put into buttered ring. Mold and bake in a pan of hot water in moderate oven about 20 minutes or until set. Unmold on platter and fill center with creamed mushrooms or peas.

CHICKEN SOUFFLE

1½ tablespoons butter	½ teaspoon salt
1½ tablespoons flour	¼ teaspoon pepper
1½ cups stock or milk	¼ teaspoon grated lemon
½ cup stale bread crumbs	rind
3 eggs	

Blend butter and flour in sauce pan without browning, add milk, stir until boiling, add salt, pepper, bread crumbs and lemon rind. Cool, then stir in the chicken. Beat yolks, add, fold in well beaten whites. Bake in a well greased pan in a moderate oven about ½ hour.

"Wavertree Hall"

CHICKEN TETRAZZINI

1¾ pound fowl cut up
2 stalks celery
1 peeled and sliced onion
1 teaspoon salt
2 tablespoons flour
Speck cayenne pepper
1 egg yolk slightly beaten
3 tablespoons top milk

1 jigger sherry
½ pound sliced washed fresh mushrooms
2 tablespoons chicken fat
1 cup fine grated cheese (Parmesan)
Chicken broth
1 cup fine noodles

1 tablespoon butter

First Process: The day before clean chicken and place in kettle with next 3 ingredients, and boiling water to cover. Simmer, covered 1-1½ hours, or until a fork can easily be inserted in the leg. Cool chicken and broth quickly. Remove skin and bones, and cut meat in strips. Strain broth. Store broth at once in refrigerator.

Second Process: Next day, melt 2 tablespoons chicken fat skimmed from broth in double boiler. Stir in flour, ½ teaspoon salt, cayenne, then 1 cup broth, cook, stirring until thickened. Slowly stir in combined egg yolks and top milk, and then slowly add the jigger of sherry. Add chicken, then mushrooms, sautéed 3 minutes in 2 tablespoons chicken fat. Heat.

Third Process: Meanwhile cook noodles tender about 10 minutes in remaining boiling chicken broth, adding water if needed. Drain; arrange ½ the noodles in bottom of shallow baking dish. Pour chicken over them, add more noodles, then more chicken. Top with cheese sprinkled over all, then dot with butter. Brown under broiler.

Add hard boiled eggs when necessary to stretch a little

further. For a special occasion dish decorate top with blanched and sliced almonds.

Serves: 6.

CHICKEN AND WALNUTS

Nanking Cook Book

1 cup shelled walnuts	1 teaspoon salt
6 mushrooms, diced	1 teaspoon sugar
1 cup chicken, diced	3 tablespoons Soy Sauce
2 tablespoons flour	(Worcestershire sauce)
3 tablespoons shortening	

Fry walnuts in deep fat until lightly brown, and drain. Place lard, or any shortening desired, in pan and slightly fry chicken, then add flour, salt, sugar and Soy Sauce which have been previously mixed together. Stir in the mushrooms, add walnuts and cook about 5 minutes. Cover and simmer for a few minutes longer. This amount is enough for 4 people and may be served with rice, or fine noodles, and shredded cabbage sautéed, for luncheon or supper.

POULET ROYAL

Cut up one cooked chicken into fairly large pieces. Put it in a good cream sauce seasoned with cheese and the yolk of one egg. Line a glass pie dish or casserole with spinach which has been cooked five to seven minutes and prepared for eating. Cover spinach with the creamed chicken, run in hot oven and serve immediately when golden brown. This dish may be varied with mushrooms, sweetbreads, etc. No quantities have been given as it can be made with whole chicken or left overs.

This recipe serves 6 persons.

CHILE

1 pound ground beef	2 onions
1 tablespoon bacon fat	2 or 3 garlic buttons
2 tablespoons chile powder	½ pint red kidney beans
Salt to taste	cooked in hot water and
1 cup tomato soup	salt

Cook meat and spices together, then add the cooked beans, and cook all together.   *"Gallison Hall"*

EGGS MARINIERE

Drop 5 or 6 eggs very carefully so as not to break into a shallow baking dish, glass preferred. In the spaces made by the whites put alternately oysters and boiled shrimps until the spaces are filled. Sprinkle lightly with salt and paprika and a dash of cayenne. Pour over all a rich white sauce, enough to moisten them well. Sprinkle with grated American cheese and small pieces of butter. Bake in oven until eggs are set. Serve at once.

EGGS SEVIGNY

6 eggs	Toast
Chicken hash	Cream sauce

Take six individual casseroles and lay a slice of buttered toast, from which the crust has been removed, in bottom of each. Cover generously with chicken hash made with cream sauce. Next, place a poached egg in each casserole and dust with salt and pepper. Pour 2 or 3 tablespoons heavy cream over egg, or use more cream sauce for this. Sprinkle generously with finely grated sharp cheese and run under broiler until cheese is melted and bubbles.

HAM, OYSTERS AND MUSHROOMS

In a frying pan frizzle 4 slices of ham; Western or Virginia Country ham, preferably the latter, may be used. Set the ham in a warming oven on plate while you brown ½ pound mushrooms in the same frying pan. To this add a pint of oysters with the oyster liquor. When oysters begin to curl add 2 tablespoons of cooking sherry and add seasoning to taste. Serve ham on slices of toasted bread and oysters and mushrooms over the ham with the gravy poured on top of all.

Serves: 4.

RISOTTO AI FUNGHI

RICE WITH MUSHROOMS

Fry in butter a piece of onion until golden color. Add fresh mushrooms cut in long and fine pieces. Add the rice, mix, cover with meat broth. Stir, add some more broth to cover when dry, and so on until done. Add a piece of butter and sprinkle with Parmesan cheese before serving. A cup of rice serves two.

RISOTTO PIEDMONTESE

2 tablespoons butter
3 chicken livers or ½ cup of lean beef
3 fresh tomatoes or 1 cup canned tomatoes

1½ cups rice
2 onions
2 cups chicken broth or stock

Put 2 tablespoons butter in sauce pan with *chicken liver*, or the same amount of chopped meat, salt and pepper. When cooked add 3 fresh tomatoes or 1 cup canned tomatoes. Cook slowly for ½ or ¾ hour. Add 1½ cups rice, cook 2 minutes in the sauce, add 2 cups chicken broth, cover and cook slowly for ½ hour. If this gets too dry, add more broth. Serve with Parmesan cheese. Enough for 6 people.

POTATOES WITH SHRIMP

Bake eight medium sized potatoes until mealy. Mash the potatoes. Add butter and cream until light and fluffy, then salt and pepper. Mash one pound, or two cans, of shrimp with the potato masher. Season with red pepper, salt, lemon juice and a pinch of horse radish. Chop very fine one-half cup of celery and celery leaves. Mix potatoes and shrimp. Stuff potato shells without packing. Dot with butter, heat in oven and serve.

MRS. CHALFIN'S STUFFED CUCUMBERS

8 medium cucumbers	Salt, pepper, celery seed to taste
1 green pepper, chopped	
½ pound pork sausage	1 teaspoon fresh thyme leaves plus a pinch of sage, unless sausage is already highly seasoned
2½ cups soft bread crumbs, or cubes	

Wipe and peel cucumbers. Cut in half lengthwise. Remove seeds and chop and drain them. Cook sausage and peppers until slightly brown. Add to the cucumber pulp without the grease. Use 2 tablespoons of this fat to make a gravy with flour and ½ cup milk. Add to the other ingredients with the bread, seasonings and herbs. Fill cucumber shells, sprinkle with chopped chives or parsley and top with melted butter. Bake at 375° F. for about ½ hour or until tops are brown and cucumbers done.

Note: Eggplant and Summer Squash are both good done this way.

STEWED KIDNEYS

3 kidneys
1½ cups consommé
1 tablespoon butter
Salt and pepper

1 sprig parsley
1 sprig thyme
1 sprig bay leaf chopped
very fine

Select perfectly fresh kidneys, wash and boil about 15 minutes. Let cool and chop fine. Put butter into sauce pan, when melted and very hot add the kidneys and chopped herbs, being careful to stir constantly to prevent burning. Add consommé and thicken with a little blended flour and butter. Just before serving, add a little sherry.

Fish and Seafood

OYSTERS BOHEMIAN

Four dozen extra large oysters. Strain and set the oyster liquid to one side. Put a large saucepan (iron) on the fire, and allow it to get hot. Then put in the oysters, and allow them to stick for a moment or so, to the hot iron. Stir and scrape up the brown portions of the oysters from the iron, and continue to let them stick, and stir, as this gives a delicious flavor of broiled oysters. Add salt. At the end of five minutes add about a cup of oyster liquor, then add a pint of rich milk. Cream a cup of butter, with two level kitchen spoonfuls of corn starch. Mix this with the yellow of two eggs, stir this into the oysters, and allow this to thicken. As soon as it is quite thick, remove from fire. In the meanwhile, boil in salt water until very tender, enough fine noodles to make, when cooked, about six large cups full and have grated a pound of American cheese. Have ready a casserole. Put in the bottom, one-third of the noodles, on top of this one-third of the oysters, ladle on to this one-third of the sauce and sprinkle heavily with American cheese. Sprinkle with black pepper. Then begin again with noodles, oysters, salt, and cheese, finally adding the third layer, which finishes the last of the ingredients. Last of all, sprinkle with black pepper. This can be put aside, not in the ice box, and run in the oven twenty minutes before serving, as it is already cooked. The object is to heat thoroughly and to make the cheese on top brown slightly.

41

ESCALLOPED OYSTERS

1 quart select oysters	1 cup bread crumbs
¼ pound butter	Salt and pepper to taste

Pick over oysters carefully; place in pan, sprinkling salt, pepper and crumbs over lightly; dot lavishly with butter. Continue until pan is full. Bake 20 minutes in quick oven. Two tablespoons cream help but are not necessary.

OYSTER FRICASSEE

1 pint oysters	¼ teaspoon salt
2 tablespoons butter	1 teaspoon chopped parsley
2 tablespoons flour	1 egg
Milk or cream	

Clean the oysters, heat oyster liquor to boiling point and strain through double thickness of cheese cloth. Add oysters to liquor and cook until plump. Remove oysters with skimmer and add enough cream to liquor to make a cupful. Melt butter, add flour, and pour on gradually hot liquid; add salt, cayenne, parsley, oysters and egg, slightly beaten.

FRIED OYSTERS

Pick over oysters to remove all pieces of shell. Drain. Sift together several times 1½ cups cracker meal, ½ cup flour, 1 teaspoon salt, 4 teaspoons baking powder (level measurements). Place this mixture on large tray or platter. Place two oysters together, with thick parts at opposite ends, in the meal. Do not let the meal get between them or they will come apart. Sprinkle meal on top and pat into shape. Fry at once in very hot deep Wesson Oil until brown.

OYSTERS LONGCHAMPS

Melt two tablespoons butter in enamel pan, cook in it a small onion chopped up and a cup of mushrooms. Thicken with two tablespoons flour and stir till flour has no lumps. When mixture is smooth add two tablespoons sherry, ½ teaspoon salt, a little red pepper, one pint oysters and a tablespoon of chopped parsley. Cook for a few minutes. Then pour into a shallow casserole, cover with bread crumbs, and brown in a moderate oven.

MINCED OYSTERS

1 quart oysters, chopped
2 egg yolks, hard boiled
1 tablespoon butter
¾ pint browned bread crumbs
2 raw egg yolks

A little chopped onion, salt, pepper, nutmeg and lemon juice.

Put all in an agate vessel until heated, then put into baking dish. Sprinkle bread crumbs over the top and bake about half an hour.

"Credenhill"

OYSTERS WITH MUSHROOMS

1 cup oysters
1 cup mushrooms, fresh, browned in 1 tablespoon butter
1½ cups milk and cream mixed
3 tablespoons flour
½ teaspoon salt
3 tablespoons butter
1 teaspoon onion juice
½ teaspoon lemon juice

Drain oysters, put them into hot pan. Cook until the edges begin to curl, then remove to hot dish. Make sauce by adding to the oyster liquor the juice from mushrooms, and enough milk to make a pint. Thicken this with the flour blended with the butter, and cook two to five minutes. Add chopped mushrooms, onion juice, lemon juice and salt. Add oysters and cook over hot water until sauce thickens, stirring constantly. Serve at once.

CRAB CAKES

1 pound crab meat	½ cup dried bread crumbs
½ cup milk	1 teaspoon flour
⅛ pound butter	Dry mustard to taste
1 egg	Salt and pepper

Scald milk. Add butter and flour to thicken. Take from stove, add crab meat, break in egg and add seasoning. Mix well. Make into cakes. Dip in beaten egg and roll in crumbs. Fry in deep fat until crisp and brown.

CRAB FLAKES AU GRATIN

1 pound crab flakes	½ pound strong cheese

Make a rich cream sauce, about 2 cups. Add cheese, dash of mustard, ½ teaspoon curry powder, several tablespoons Worcestershire sauce, salt, pepper, and chopped chives. Pour crab flakes into hot sauce, mix well, and put into baking dish. Cover with browned bread crumbs which have been dipped in melted butter. Heat thoroughly in oven.

MILLER AND RHOADS DEVILED CRAB

1 pound crab meat	Few drops of tabasco sauce
1 tablespoon butter	1 teaspoon Worcestershire
½ cup heavy cream sauce	sauce
Salt to taste	

Clean shell, mix ingredients together and place in shell. Wipe top with beaten egg, particularly over the part where the filling and shell join to prevent fat from soaking into the filling, and finally dust carefully with buttered bread crumbs or cracker meal.

Fry in deep fryer at 375° F. or 380° F. for 1 minute, or until golden brown.

SOFT SHELL CRABS

Clean crabs, sprinkle with salt and pepper, dip in crumbs, egg, and crumbs, fry in deep fat and drain. Being light, they will rise to top of fat and should be turned while frying. Soft shell crabs are usually fried. Serve with Sauce Tartare.

To clean a crab: Lift and fold back the tapering points which are found on each side of the back shell and remove spongy substance that lies under them. Turn crab on its back and with a pointed knife remove the small piece at lower part of shell, which terminates in a point; this is called the apron.

SEA FOOD CASSEROLE

1 pound lobster claw or tail meat

1 pound crab meat

1 pound cooked shelled shrimp

1 pound scallops, cooked in white dry wine and halved

SAUCE

¼ pound butter

10 tablespoons flour

1 pint cream

1½ cups consommé

¼ teaspoon cayenne pepper

1 tablespoon horseradish

2 teaspoons French mustard

2 tablespoons ketchup

¼ cup sherry

2 cloves garlic, grated

Juice of ½ lime

1 teaspoon salt

2 teaspoons monosodium glutamate

¼ cup chopped parsley

Melt the butter, add the flour. and slowly add the

cream and consommé, which have been heated. When completely smooth, add all seasonings except parsley. Add the sea food and sherry, and rectify the seasoning. If the sauce is too thick, thin with a little milk; if too thin, thicken with a little cornstarch smoothed with milk. Turn into a casserole and set aside until about one-half hour before serving time. Heat in a moderate oven, 350° F., for one-half hour. Before serving, sprinkle with parsley. This dish is good accompanied by a dish of fresh peas and sautéed mushrooms, bacon biscuit, two crisp vegetable relishes.

Serves: 8.

ROE HERRING

A real Virginia breakfast dish is Roe Herring served with batterbread or corn cakes and sorghum.

This is not the usual salt herring found in most parts of the country, but the herrings caught and put in brine in the spring when fat with roe. They seem to be prepared in this way only around the Chesapeake Bay areas and Albemarle Sound in North Carolina, but can be, and often are, shipped in small kegs for special orders to many parts of the country. When cooked, the flesh is quite red and has a distinctive flavor, and the roe itself is quite a delicacy.

Soak the herring overnight. Scrape off any extra scales, dry, dip in cornmeal and fry in small amount of bacon fat in heavy pan about 15 minutes, turning to brown on both sides.

One Roe Herring will serve 2 people usually, although some families like one apiece! It is very rich and will make you very thirsty for the rest of the day, but is quite worth it!

TO BAKE A SHAD

The shad is a very indifferent fish unless it be large and fat; when you get a good one, prepare it nicely, put some forcemeat inside, and lay it at full length in a pan with a pint of water, a gill of red wine, one of mushroom catsup, a little pepper, vinegar, salt, a few cloves of garlic, and six cloves; stew it gently until the gravy is sufficiently reduced; there should always be a fish-slice with holes to lay the fish on, for the convenience of dishing without breaking it; when the fish is taken up, slip it carefully into the dish; thicken the gravy with butter and brown flour, and pour over it.

From: *"The Virginia Housewife"*
by Mrs. Mary Randolph
Fourth Edition—1830

BAKED STUFFED SHAD

Buy a nice firm, fat Roe Shad about 3-4 pounds. Remove roe, stuff cavity with a good, well-seasoned poultry stuffing and sew up loosely. Place in a greased baking dish after seasoning with salt and pepper, put several strips of bacon across the shad, place in a 400° F. oven and bake about an hour, basting occasionally. Thirty minutes before it is done, place the well-seasoned roe in the pan and baste with drippings. Serve whole, garnished with lemon.

FRIED SHAD

Have a shad split and large bones removed. Cut halves into about 3-4 sections each. Season with salt and pepper, dip in cornmeal, and fry until golden brown in a heavy pan, using bacon fat. Takes about 10-15 minutes, turning once.

SHRIMP A LA CREOLE

1 pound fresh shrimp or 1   1 large onion
   can of shrimp   1 sweet pepper
            1 small can tomatoes

Chop onion fine and brown in ½ cup of olive oil or other fat, add tomatoes and some celery and parsley chopped fine, salt and pepper to taste. Stew down and add shrimp. Thicken this with a little flour and brown. Worcestershire sauce is nice in this. Serve with rice, cooked dry.

SOLE MARGUERY

Filet of sole   ¼ cup soft butter
Shrimps   Few mussels or oysters
4 egg yolks   Sliced mushrooms
           ½ cup cream

Season filet with salt and pepper, place in pan with mussels or oysters, shrimps and mushrooms, cover generously with white wine. Cook slowly for 10 minutes, pour sauce off fish into top of double boiler, there should be 1 cupful, add cream and allow the mixture to reduce to ½ quantity, add yolks of eggs, stir briskly until eggs are thick, add gradually the soft butter and stir until smooth. Pour sauce over fish, serve at once.

DELICIOUS COLD SALMON

Wrap 4 pounds or more salmon (one piece, or one fish) in cheesecloth. Steam for 6 minutes per pound, covered, in broth made from one and a half cups water, one onion, one piece celery, the juice of one lemon and two teaspoons salt. Turn once. Cool enough to handle carefully. Remove cheesecloth and slip out back bone and scrape off skin. Chill, and serve with hard boiled eggs and Hollandaise sauce.

"Tall Pines"

"JO'S FISH DISH"

Melt 2 tablespoons butter. Stir into it ¼ cup fresh bread crumbs and 2/3 cup milk. Boil 5 minutes, stirring constantly. Add 1 cup flaked fish (tuna, salmon or leftovers) and 2 eggs slightly beaten, ½ teaspoon salt, 1 tablespoon chopped parsley and the juice of one lemon. Turn into buttered ring mold and cover with buttered paper. Bake in pan of hot water in moderate oven for 30 minutes. Turn out and fill center with creamed peas and mushrooms.

"Tall Pines"

Meats and Poultry

COOKING VIRGINIA HAM

Scrub ham thoroughly and put in large kettle with cold water to cover. Let water come to boil, but keep it at the just barely moving point, cooking until the bone is loose and skin is puffed and wrinkled. This slow boil is very important for a good texture of the meat. Cool in water in which it was cooked, take skin off, sprinkle bread crumbs and a little brown sugar on top and stick with cloves. Return to oven, bake to nice brown. Let get very cold before cutting and cut wafer thin.

"Ingleside"

JAMBALYA

1 cup chopped ham	½ can tomatoes
1½ cups hot water or stock	1 cup rice
1 chicken cooked, or scraps of chicken or other meat	

Melt a tablespoon of lard in a pot, brown a cut-up onion in this, add a spoon of flour to brown, and one-half can of tomatoes, already heated. Add ham and other meat which have already been cooked, season with salt, pepper, sweet pepper and paprika.

Put one and one-half cups of hot water or stock in this and cook ten minutes. Add one cup of rice and cook until this is done. If you have uncooked chicken for this, fry brown first, then boil tender, using this stock.

FRIED CHICKEN

One 1½ to 2½ pound young chicken

Salt, pepper, flour
Fat for frying

The butcher will clean and cut up your chicken into frying size pieces. Dry it well, put into a paper bag with ½ cup flour, salt and pepper to taste, and shake till each piece is well dusted.

In the meantime, have heating a large heavy skillet (the old fashioned black iron kind is perfect) with fat about ¾ of an inch deep; either Wesson Oil, Crisco, or lard. When good and hot add the pieces of chicken, being careful not to overcrowd the pan. Turn down the heat slightly, and brown to a golden brown on all sides, turning each piece several times in the process. This should take about 15 minutes. Then do either of two things:

Drain off the excess fat, cover *loosely* with light weight lid, turn down heat and cook very slowly, another 15 to 20 minutes, until tender, being careful not to burn it or let the steam make the crust soggy; or

Remove the pieces from the skillet to a shallow pan, cover loosely, and put in a slow oven to cook the last 15 or 20 minutes. If in the process of tenderizing the crust should become soggy it may be re-crisped in a hot oven.

The gravy is made from the last 2 or 3 tablespoons of fat and the rich brown crumbs in the bottom of the skillet with the remaining flour from the bag and either water or milk. The milk gravy is a favorite with fried chicken in the South.

Serve the chicken heaped in a platter, with gravy in a separate bowl, *never* poured around the chicken.

PORK CHOPS IN VERMOUTH

4 loin chops cut 1½ inches thick   1 clove garlic

Paprika   ½ cup stock or consommé

Sage   ½ cup dry French vermouth

Salt   ½-1 cup sour cream (optional)

In a heavy iron pan, brown chops heavily. Dust upper sides with paprika, salt, and a little sage. Add stock and garlic, cover and simmer on top of stove or in a 300° F. oven until tender, or about an hour. Remove chops to heatproof serving dish. Add vermouth to the juices in the pan, and sour cream, if desired. Stir thoroughly and pour over chops. Heat for about 15 minutes, turning and basting chops.

Veal cutlet can be cooked the same way, substituting chervil or thyme for the sage.

SPARERIBS

Take young pork spareribs, and after wiping them off with a damp cloth, put them on the broiler quite near the flame. Have the oven set for broiling temperature. Now, take 2 or 3 tablespoons of white or brown sugar and tie up in a cloth bag. After the meat has started to sear, dip this bag in vinegar and rub it over the spareribs every few minutes, dipping the sugar bag in vinegar repeatedly. Then turn the meat over and continue doing the same on that side until spareribs are done. Season to taste if you like, but it is not necessary as the sweet-sour basting, quite by itself, imparts a delicious and unusual flavor.

CASSEROLE OF BEEF

1 pound top round steak cut in one-inch cubes

½ cup vinegar

3 drops tabasco

1 glass water

2 tablespoonsful Worcestershire sauce

4 tablespoonsful tomato catsup

2 tablespoonsful olive oil

Pepper and salt to taste

Place meat in casserole. Pour over it the mixture made of other ingredients and sprinkle well with flour. Cover with top and bake in slow oven.

BEEF STRAGANOFF

1½ pounds round steak cut into inch cubes, or, half inch cubes if preferable

½ pound butter

¾ pound fresh mushrooms

½ cup chopped celery

½ cup chopped onions

1 cup canned tomatoes

1 tablespoon vinegar

1 tablespoon Worcestershire

1 pint sour cream

Salt and pepper to taste

1 pound rice

Shake steak in paper bag with enough flour to cover pieces well. Sauté in half the butter and remove to heavy pan. Add butter to what is left in skillet and sauté mushrooms, onion and celery. Add to steak mixture. Wash skillet with tomatoes and add to steak. Cover and cook for two hours, or until meat is very tender. Add cream, vinegar and sauce, and season with additional salt, if necessary. Serve on fluffy rice.

This is fine for buffet suppers.

"Tall Pines"

BOEUF A LA MODE

4 to 5 pounds boneless pot roast

A little fat pork

1 tablespoonful salt

Pepper to taste

1 pint dry red wine

2 tablespoonsful each, fat and flour

Veal knuckle bone

12 small onions browned in butter

1 quart stock or water

1 cup canned tomatoes

1 clove garlic and a dash of thyme

½ bay leaf

Few sprigs parsley, stalk of celery and leek tied together

5-6 carrots cut in pieces

Lard roast with pork, season with salt and pepper, soak in wine in refrigerator for six hours, turning several times. Dry meat well and brown in fat. Drain off fat when roast is brown. Sprinkle flour in bottom of kettle and mix with brown juice from meat. Add bone, wine, stock, tomatoes, garlic and herbs. Meat should be *just* covered. Bring to boil, reduce heat and cook slowly on top burner or in oven at 350° F., 3 to 4 hours until tender. Remove meat and bone, skim fat, and strain gravy. Clean pan and put back meat with carrots, onions and gravy. Simmer 20 to 30 minutes until the vegetables are tender. Taste for seasoning.

Serve hot the first day. For the second serving, slice remainder meat, put in loaf pan, pour gravy over and refrigerate. It will jell and can be served as aspic.

SIRLOIN TIP IN RED WINE

4 pound sirloin tip cut in 1 inch slices

1 cup flour

1 teaspoon saffron

2 teaspoonsful monosodium glutamate

4 tablespoonsful paprika
2 teaspoonsful salt
1 teaspoon pepper
1 teaspoon sweet basil

3-4 cloves finely chopped garlic
1 can consommé
1½ cups dry red wine

Bacon fat

Cut the slices of sirloin into one-inch cubes. Make a broth of the trimmings. Put into a paper bag the flour, paprika, salt, and pepper. Drop in the beef and shake, coating each piece thoroughly. Brown the meat in hot bacon fat in an iron pan. The meat must be heavily browned. Remove the meat to an earthenware casserole. Empty the frying pan of excess fat, but do not scrape it. Replace on heat and add the consommé, basil, saffron, garlic, and monosodium glutamate. Bring this mixture to a boil and pour over meat in casserole. Add enough of the wine almost to cover and cook in a 300° F. oven until tender. This should take from 2 to 3 hours. As the liquid evaporates, add wine and broth from scraps. Good with a green vegetable and hot buttered French bread.

Serves: 8.

HOT SMOKED TONGUE

1 smoked tongue, 3-4 pounds
Whole cloves

1 glass blackberry jelly
Juice of 1 lemon

1 cup raisins

Boil tongue in water to cover to which add stalk of celery, 1 sliced onion, 1 bay leaf, 1 carrot, 1 tablespoon mixed spices. Cook until tender, about 3-4 hours. Cool in water in which it has been cooked. Remove skin and trim off fat and gristle. Stick with cloves, dust with flour, pour over all the jelly beaten soft with lemon juice, and raisins which have been cooked tender in a cup of water. Bake in hot oven at 400° F. for 30 minutes, basting often. Serve hot.

Serves 5 or 6.

BARBECUED LAMB FROM ALABAMA

4-5 pound leg of lamb	4 tablespoonsful tomato
6 cupfuls water	ketchup
¼ cup vinegar	2 tablespoonsful sugar
2 onions	2 tablespoonsful Worcester-
Flour	shire sauce
½ teaspoonful dry mustard	Salt and pepper to taste

Salt and pepper lamb and roll in flour. Put in roaster. Add chopped onions and pour all other ingredients over meat. Put on lid of roaster and bake in a moderate, 350° F., oven for 3-4 hours or until meat is tender. Meat should be turned and basted with sauce in roaster every half-hour. Remove top from roaster one-half hour before meat is ready, to permit browning. Serve with sauce in roaster.

COSTOLETTE DE AGNELLO

LAMB CUTLETS

Fry in butter the cutlets until golden brown. Add meat broth and water to cover. Dissolve in water a spoonful of fecula. Add to the cutlets a piece of garlic, parsley chopped fine, and mushrooms cut in little pieces. Cook for 45 minutes. Add lemon juice before serving.

VEAL ALTROCCHI

1½ pounds veal	Salt and pepper
4 tablespoonsful olive oil	1 cup finely chopped
1 tablespoonful vinegar	parsley
Flour	

Have the butcher cut veal from leg after cutlets have

been removed. The slices should be about the size of the palm of a small hand, about one-half an inch thick. Dip them in flour which has been well-seasoned with salt and freshly ground black pepper. Heat the olive oil until it starts to smoke a little. Add the vinegar. Brown veal lightly, pushing pieces to edge of pan as they brown. This will take only 10-12 minutes. When all are brown, add the parsley and stir until all is well-mixed.

This may be served as it is on a hot platter or on a bed of rice.

VEAL CASSEROLE

2 pounds veal cutlet	Salt and pepper
2 tablespoonsful butter	1 cup cream
Flour	Sherry

Cut veal in two-inch cubes, dredge with flour and brown in butter. Put in casserole and cover tightly. Cook about one-half hour in oven or until tender. Add cream and cook ten minutes longer. Thicken with flour and water, and add sherry and any other seasonings needed.

"Hollymead"

VEAL EN DAUBE

A 5-pound boned roast of veal, preferably from the loin. Make deep incisions every inch or so in the roast and stuff each one with a small piece of bacon, a bit of dried red pepper, and a small sliver of garlic. Dredge roast in flour to which thyme, sage, salt and pepper have been added. Brown in hot bacon fat in an iron pan.

In an iron Dutch oven, brown in bacon fat 1 chopped onion, 2 chopped carrots, 2 chopped turnips, 2 stalks celery chopped, 1 green pepper chopped. When lightly brown, add roast and enough dry wine to prevent scorching. Cover and simmer gently until tender.

This is good hot served with a sauce made of the sieved vegetables and juices. It is, however, a much better dish served cold.

GRILLADES

2 pounds veal ½ can of tomatoes
2 cups of water

Make a roux of one tablesoonful of lard or butter and two tablespoonfuls of browned flour. Add the water, hot, slowly and season with onion, bay leaf, green pepper, salt, pepper, and a little thyme. Add tomatoes and stew. Fry the veal, cut into pieces the proper size to serve, and add. Let cook one-half hour and serve.

RUMP OR SHOULDER OF VEAL
TO BE ROLLED

First rub inside of veal thoroughly with clove garlic. Sprinkle with chopped parsley and grated onion and dash of salt and pepper. Smear with butter. Roll veal and tie with string. Smear with butter and seasoning on outside, having a *good coating* of butter. Put in uncovered roasting pan with 2 tablespoonfuls of butter and put in hot oven until golden brown, then pour glass of water into pan. Cover pan, reduce heat, and cook until done. Keep hot while you add to juices in pan one tumbler of milk and small piece of butter. Pour over meat and serve.

STUFFED VEAL CHOPS

Get the desired number of veal chops one inch thick, compact and uniform in size. Have the butcher gash them ready to be stuffed. Fill the cavity with a dressing of bread crumbs, a little chopped green pepper, onion, and celery, pepper and salt to taste, and moistened with a little melted butter. Rub flour, salt, and pepper on both sides of the chops, and brown in hot butter. Then lower heat, add a little water to the pan, cover tightly, and cook about 30 minutes, basting frequently. More water may be added as necessary. These must cook slowly to be good.

HOW TO COOK A PARTRIDGE

Pick dry. Wash but do not soak in water. Wipe dry. Put two small slices of fat meat in pan, lay bird on this, breast up, no water. Make a sauce of melted butter, vinegar, red pepper, and salt. Pour this over the bird and steam until done.

CHICKEN CROQUETTES

2 cups thick white sauce	1 tablespoonful chopped
1 quart chicken cut fine or	parsley
put through meat grinder	1 teaspoonful lemon juice
Salt and pepper to taste	

Mix well together. Make into croquettes and roll in cracker crumbs. Keep in ice box at least four hours. One hour before frying roll in beaten egg and cracker crumbs.

WHITE SAUCE

1/3 cup butter	1 cup milk and 1 cup rich
6 level tablespoonsful flour	stock

Melt butter, add flour, then add liquid slowly, stirring constantly.

Note: Other meats, such as lamb, etc., may be used.

PICKLED CHICKEN

3 chickens, about 2 pounds each
1½ cups vinegar
½ cup water
½ bottle of Worcestershire sauce

1 tablespoon sugar
¼ pound butter for each chicken
Onion rings sliced over chickens
Salt and pepper

Put in pan in *low* oven. Cook 3-4 hours, basting frequently.

ARROZ CON POLLO

CHICKEN AND RICE SPANISH STYLE

3 tablespoonsful olive oil
1 tablespoon vinegar
3 tiny black peppers
1 clove
1 laurel leaf
Chicken stock to cover rice

3 small tomatoes
1 pinch saffron
1 sweet red pepper
3 garlic buttons
1 onion
1 handful rice to each person

Pimentos to decorate

Cut up a two-pound spring chicken and put it on to boil in hot water and salt. While it is cooking, put vinegar, black peppers, clove, laurel leaf, red pepper, garlic, onion and tomatoes in the casserole and fry them in the olive oil. When the chicken is rather tender, put it into the casserole with the spices and brown slightly, and then add the rice and enough chicken stock to cover the rice. As the rice absorbs the liquid add more chicken stock or boiling water. When the rice is about half cooked, diminish fire, add the Spanish saffron, crushed and dissolved in a little hot water, and let all cook slowly until sufficiently but not too well-done. Garnish with slices of Spanish pimentos and sprinkling of green peas, and serve from the casserole.

"Gallison Hall"

Vegetables

JERUSALEM ARTICHOKES

These are boiled and dressed in the various ways we have just before directed for potatoes. They should be covered with thick melted butter or a nice white or brown sauce.

"The Virginia Housewife"
by Mrs. Mary Randolph
Fourth Edition, Published 1830

STRING BEANS

French slice young, tender string beans and cook for 15 minutes, or until just tender, in small amount of salted water. Drain and pour over them hot French dressing and sprinkle with bits of crisp bacon.

ASPARAGUS WITH ALMONDS

Make a cream sauce by adding flour to melted butter, salt and pepper and milk. Add one-half cup of blanched almonds. Put layer of canned asparagus in greased baking dish, alternating each layer with above sauce. Put buttered bread crumbs on top and bake until brown.

ASPARAGUS SOUFFLE

Chop fine 2 cans asparagus, season with salt and pepper, add 1½ tablespoons sugar, 1 cup bread crumbs, 1 cup cream sauce, and the yolks of 4 eggs. Mix and bake 1 hour in a casserole, which has previously been placed in a pan of hot water. Stir occasionally. Fold in the beaten whites of the 4 eggs and bake 15 minutes

63

longer. When ready to serve, cover with whipped cream garnished with paprika.

CARROT FRITTERS

2 cups mashed cooked car- 2 eggs
  rots   ½ teaspoon salt

To the mashed carrots add salt and egg yolks, well-beaten. Beat the white of eggs until stiff and fold into the mixture. Heat the heavy iron skillet or griddle and grease well with fat. Drop mixture by spoonful upon griddle and cook until well-browned on each side.

ANNIE'S CORN PUDDING

3 eggs   1 pint of milk
2 tablespoons flour   1 tablespoon sugar
1 teaspoon salt   Butter size of an egg,
1½ cups corn freshly   melted
  scraped from cob

Mix eggs and flour together until smooth, add milk and melted butter. Put in the other ingredients and bake in well-greased baking pan about 30 minutes.

CREAMED CYMLINGS

Cut white or yellow cymlings into pieces, peeling skin off only if it is tough. Boil in as small amount of salted water as possible until it is tender. Mash through a potato masher, draining all surplus water possible. Return to heavy pan, add a generous amount of butter and enough top milk and cream to make the cymlings fairly liquid. Season with salt, black pepper and dash of red pepper to taste. Cook over very low fire without a lid, stirring frequently until cymlings are thick as soft, mashed potatoes.

CYMLING PUDDING

Wash, but do not peel, slice, and cook in cold water 3 or 4 small, yellow crooked-neck cymlings (squash). Add, while cooking, ½ teaspoon salt, ½ teaspoon sugar, and if desired, ½ small chopped onion. Boil ten minutes, or until tender. Drain, then mash with potato masher. Add 1½ tablespoons butter, 1 cup rich milk, or thick cream, which has been beaten with 1 egg. Pour into buttered casserole and bake like a corn pudding in a pan of warm water at about 400° F. oven temperature.

STUFFED CYMLINGS OR SMALL SUMMER SQUASH

Boil four cymlings or squash until a fork penetrates fairly easily and yet not quite done. Cut slices off top and with a spoon, spoon out insides, leaving a shell to be stuffed. Then using the frying pan in which your breakfast bacon was fried, with an additional good tablespoon of the bacon fat, fry one good sized finely cut up onion. Add the strained and mashed insides of your squash with a tablespoon of cream and season to taste with salt and pepper and Worcestershire sauce. Put this back into the shells and top with cracker and bread crumbs mixed, then a grating of cheese and dot with butter and sprinkle with paprika. Bake until brown, or run under broiler.
Oven: 400. Time: 15-20 minutes. Serves: 4.

EGGPLANT PUDDING

1 eggplant	½ finely chopped onion
½ teaspoon salt	2 egg yolks, slightly beaten
1 teaspoon chopped parsley	3 tablespoons cooked rice
2 tablespoons butter	Bread crumbs

Cook eggplant 15 minutes in boiling salted water. Cut

slice from top and remove pulp, being careful not to break skin. Cook onion in butter for 5 minutes, add seasoning and rice and mix with bread crumbs. Bake for 25 minutes in a moderate oven. A little vegetable stock or cream may be used if the filling is not soft enough.

ONIONS AND PECANS

Skin and cook one quart silver skinned onions until just barely done, pouring off water after they first come to boil and covering with fresh water, to which salt and a small amount of sugar have been added. Drain on brown paper or in collander until very dry. Arrange in baking dish, sprinkle with a cup of shelled pecans, unbroken, and pour over all a cream sauce. Cream sauce should be made with top milk to which a little sugar has been added. Sprinkle with buttered bread crumbs and bake in a moderate oven until brown. This can be fixed well ahead of time and browned at the last minute.

ITALIAN SPINACH BALLS

Cook spinach, drain, and put through meat chopper. Season with salt, pepper, and nutmeg. Add enough egg and flour to mold into balls or croquettes. Drop into boiling water and cook for ten minutes. Serve hot with melted butter and Parmesan cheese.

BROILED TOMATOES

Select large, firm tomatoes and do not peel. Slice one-half an inch thick and broil. A few minutes will suffice to cook them. Have ready in a cup some melted butter seasoned with pepper, salt, a little sugar and one-half teaspoon of made mustard. As soon as the tomatoes are done, dip each piece in this mixture and lay upon a hot dish. When all are dished, heat what remains of the seasoning to a boil, pour upon them and serve at once.

BAKED TOMATOES STUFFED WITH MUSHROOMS

4 medium tomatoes
¾ cup (about 8 small) sliced mushrooms
2 tablespoons melted butter or margarine
1 tablespoon finely chopped onion

2 tablespoons flour
½ teaspoon salt
Dash of pepper
½ cup milk
2 tablespoons fine dry bread crumbs

Remove tops from stem ends of tomatoes. Carefully scoop out pulp and juice and reserve it. Slice mushrooms and brown in butter or margarine with onion. Blend in flour, salt, and pepper. Remove from heat, add milk and stir until smooth. Add ¾ cup of the reserve tomato juice and pulp, cut in small pieces. Cook, stirring constantly, about five minutes or until thick. Place tomato shells in shallow baking dish. Fill with mushroom and tomato sauce. Sprinkle with bread crumbs. Bake 12 to 15 minutes in a hot oven, 400° F., or until tomatoes are tender.

FRIED TOMATOES WITH CREAM SAUCE

Select six green or moderately ripe tomatoes. Cut in one-half inch slices. Roll in flour to which has been added salt and pepper. Put 2 tablespoons of butter in pan and melt. Add 1½ tablespoons of flour, ½ onion sliced. Cook onion until it is a light brown. Brown the tomatoes in this mixture. Remove the tomatoes to thin slices of toast. Add to the onion mixture, one cup of milk, ½ cup of cream. When thick as cream, pour over the tomatoes and toast. Serve very hot.

Note: Bacon grease can be used instead of butter.

"STICKY" TOMATOES

6 good sized ripe tomatoes
　or one can of tomatoes
1 teacup of bread crumbs

2 teacups of sugar
1 tablespoon of butter
Pinch of salt and pepper

Put tomatoes, after peeling, in baking dish. Cover with bread crumbs, then put in sugar, add butter, salt and pepper. Stir well and put in slow oven, and cook for at least three hours.

"Woodville"

SOUTHERN OKRA WITH TOMATOES

1 slice bacon cut up or 2
　tablespoons bacon drip-
　pings
½ cup minced onion
2 cups okra cut in ½ inch
　slices

1 cup boiling water
3 cups fresh tomatoes
1½ teaspoons salt
Speck pepper
½ teaspoon granulated sugar

In nine inch skillet, fry bacon until golden, remove pieces, leaving fat in skillet. Sauté onion tender in this fat, then return bacon pieces to skillet. Add remaining ingredients. Cover, bring to boil, then turn heat low and simmer 15 to 20 minutes until tender. Stir occasionally to prevent sticking.

Serves: 4.

CANDIED SWEET POTATOES

Peel and slice raw sweet potatoes. If small, cut in half or in very thick slices. Arrange in flat, open pan. Add ½ cup brown sugar, 1 tablespoon powdered cinnamon, and good sized lump of butter. Cook slowly on top of stove or in oven. Keep covered until done through, turning potatoes constantly until clear and liquid very thick. Allow to brown off, remove to flat dish and serve hot.

SWEET POTATO SURPRISE

2 cups riced sweet potatoes, about 3 medium-sized potatoes
1 egg beaten lightly

Dash of pepper
8 marshmallows
½ teaspoon salt
½ cup crushed cornflakes

Boil and peel the potatoes, put through the ricer and when partly cool, add egg, salt and pepper. Flour the hands if necessary, form into 8 balls, concealing the marshmallows in the balls. Roll in cornflakes, then fry in hot Crisco until brown. Drain on soft paper. Canned sweet potatoes are just as good for the Surprise as fresh potatoes.

The Lawn

SALSIFY CAKES

4 cups salsify, well mashed
1 cup very fine, dry bread crumbs
1 teaspoon salt

¼ teaspoon pepper
1 teaspoon sugar
1 tablespoon vinegar
1 tablespoon melted butter

2 eggs, well beaten

Mix all ingredients together thoroughly. Fashion into flat cakes and fry.

PICKLED SALSIFY

Wash and cook in skins a bunch of nice fat salsify, or oyster plant. When tender, cool, and rub off skin and cut into thin rounds. In sauce pan put 1/3 cup brown sugar packed tight, 3 tablespoons vinegar, 1 tablespoon butter, and salt and pepper to taste. Use lots of pepper.

Add salsify and cook slowly a long time until the syrup is dark brown and sticky and the pieces thoroughly pickled. The proportions of the sauce may be varied as suits your own taste.

This is a nice "side dish", particularly in the fall served with pork loin or spareribs.

MIXED VEGETABLES

6 green peppers	6 onions
12 tomatoes	6 okra

Peel onions and tomatoes. Slice each vegetable separately. Grease a baking dish with bacon drippings. Then arrange each vegetable in layers, salt and pepper to taste. Put bread crumbs on top, and a little more of the bacon drippings. Bake slowly about an hour and serve as a vegetable. It is particularly good with steak.

"Cloverfields"

BAKED CURRY ONION

1 pound sliced onion	¼ teaspoon paprika
3 tablespoons butter	½ cup soup stock
2 tablespoons flour	½ cup milk
¼ teaspoon cayenne pepper	1 ounce grated cheese
¼ teaspoon curry powder	Salt and pepper to taste

Boil onions 15 minutes, drain and put in baking dish. Cover with sauce made of above ingredients and bake in a moderate oven about 45 minutes.

Salads

EAST INDIAN SALAD

2 cups cream cheese
1 cup grated American cheese
1 cup cream
¾ tablespoon granulated or package powdered gelatin

Tomatoes
Cucumbers
Celery
Apples

Work two cream cheeses until smooth, moistening with milk or cream. Add American cheese, one cup of cream, granulated gelatin soaked in one tablespoonful of cold water and dissolved in one tablespoonful of hot milk. Season lightly with salt and paprika and turn into a ring mold. When firm, turn out on lettuce and fill center with mayonnaise salad, tomatoes, cucumbers, celery and apples.

Serves 6 nicely.

COTTAGE CHEESE SALAD

1 stalk celery, cut small
1½ cups pecans, cut small
2 envelopes gelatin
1 pint whipped cream
¼ teaspoon salt

1¼ green peppers, cut small
1 large can pineapple, cut small
¾ cup mayonnaise
1 pint cottage cheese

Dissolve gelatin in one-quarter of the pineapple juice, cold. Then heat remaining juice and pour over it and set aside to cool. Mix thoroughly the pineapple, nuts, celery, and peppers with the cottage cheese and mayonnaise. Sweeten whipped cream with ¼ cup of sugar and fold in. Turn into molds and let stand until firm. Serve on lettuce with mayonnaise and a dash of paprika.

Serves 18-24.

"Retreat"

POTATO SALAD

1 dozen potatoes	About 18 tablespoons olive
4 teaspoons salt	oil
2 saltspoons black pepper	6 tablespoons vinegar
1½ tablespoons chopped	3 small onions, chopped fine
parsley	

Three or four slices of breakfast bacon cut thin, fried crisp, and chopped up. Peel and boil the potatoes. While warm, cut in small pieces and pour the oil over them. Put the salt and pepper in a bowl and add vinegar. Sprinkle the bacon, onions, and parsley through the potatoes, then add the vinegar, salt, and pepper that have been mixed. Mix well, garnish with parsley or lettuce and keep in cool place until ready to serve.

PLANTATION GARDEN'S TOMATO ASPIC WITH HERBS

Using a thick purée of tomatoes, for which plum tomatoes are ideal, heat 1½ cups to boiling point. Meanwhile, dissolve 1 tablespoon gelatin in ½ cup cold water. Add hot purée and stir well. Cool. Chop the following: ½ cup green pepper and celery mixed, 1 teaspoon thyme leaves, ½ teaspoon sweet basil, a few chives, 1 tablespoon parsley. Mix in with the tomato gelatin adding a little salt and celery seed, if desired. Put in refrigerator to congeal.

MOLDED CHICKEN SALAD

1 hen, boiled, cut fine (4 cups)
2 cups celery, cut fine
1 cup nuts, cut fine, preferably pecans
4 hard boiled eggs, chopped
1 can midget peas

1 tablespoon capers
2 tablespoons Worcestershire sauce
2 tablespoons chow chow pickle, chopped fine
1 pint mayonnaise
Salt to taste

Dissolve two packages of gelatin in one cup stock and when cool, stir in mayonnaise and dry ingredients. Mold in two bread pans, chill, and serve on lettuce. This serves 30 people.

SALMON IN CUCUMBER ASPIC

4 cucumbers
1 onion
1 quart water
½ teaspoon salt

2 tablespoons gelatin
½ cup cold water
1 cup flaked salmon
⅛ teaspoon white pepper
Radishes

Peel cucumbers and onion. Slice. Add salt and pepper, then the quart of water. Let the mixture simmer for one hour. Next strain and pour over gelatin, which has been thoroughly dissolved. This mixture is then left to cool until it begins to thicken. When about the consistency of molasses, the salmon is added and mixture is then turned into molds to finish stiffening. Serve with mayonnaise.

"Cismont Manor"

SHAD ROE MOLD

½ pound shade roe
1½ tablespoons gelatin
1 can consommé

1 teaspoon salt
1 tablespoon lemon juice
½ cup mayonnaise

Boil the shad roe, drain and remove skin and separate

with fork. Moisten gelatin in cold water and dissolve in hot consommé. Then add to this salt and lemon juice. Add to this mixture the mayonnaise, beating with egg beater and then add shad roe, stirring occasionally until thick. Pour in fish mold, chill, and serve as salad.

GINGER ALE SALAD

Dissolve 1 package of lime jello in ½ cup of boiling water, stirring constantly. Cool, and add 1½ cups of ginger ale. Let thicken a little, then add 1 cup of chopped nuts and celery, 1 cup of orange segments, white grapes and pineapple chunks. Fill individual molds, after dipping them in cold water, and put in ice box to congeal. Serve on lettuce with mayonnaise.

SALAD SPONGE DELIGHT

1 envelope gelatin
¼ cup cold water
¼ cup canned pineapple or cherry juice or any fruit juice
¼ pound almonds, or other nuts
¼ teaspoon salt
½ cup white grapes, or strawberries
¼ pound marshmallows
1 cup canned white cherries
1 cup cream, whipped
2 egg whites

Pour cold water in bowl and sprinkle gelatin on top of water. Add hot pineapple juice and stir until dissolved. When cold, whip with egg beater and add chopped almonds, salt, and marshmallows, grapes and cherries cut up. Fold in whipped cream, and last, whites of eggs stiffly beaten. Turn into mold that has been rinsed in cold water and chill. Use any vegetable coloring if desired. When firm, unmold and serve with whipped cream salad dressing.

JACK'S SALAD

2 heads of lettuce
4 pieces of toast
2 boxes of Kraft's Parmesan
  cheese, large size
2 lemons, juice

1 tablespoon of Worcestershire sauce
2 large sections, or 3 small,
  of garlic
Salt and pepper

1 raw egg

Cut up garlic real fine and put into about 1 small cup of Wesson Oil, and let stand for ½ to ¾ hour.

Wash and prepare lettuce, placing in large bowl, to which add in order named, dry toast cut into squares the size of croutons, the juice of the 2 lemons, Worcestershire sauce, salt and pepper to taste. Then mash garlic in oil and strain oil over salad. Break 1 raw egg over contents, and toss salad until thoroughly mixed. Add cheese, and toss until thoroughly marinated. Serve at once.

BOILED DRESSING FOR COLE SLAW

To one tablespoon of melted butter add level tablespoon of flour, mix and add one cup milk, two egg yolks beaten, one-third cup vinegar, one-third cup sugar, one-half teaspoon mustard, one-half teaspoon salt, and one-half teaspoon celery seed. Boil slowly, stirring. If it curdles, beat with rotary egg-beater.

SOUR CREAM DRESSING

4 tablespoons of salad oil
Yolks of 2 hard boiled eggs
¼ teaspoon of mustard

2 tablespoons of sugar
Salt and red pepper to taste
2 tablespoons of vinegar

½ cup of thick sour cream

Mash yolks with sugar, mustard, salt and pepper.

When smooth add oil, then vinegar, and cream last. A little of the chopped white of egg may be added. This is better if made a few hours before using. It is good on plain leaf lettuce or tomato, and is a nice sandwich dressing.

MAYONNAISE WITH BUTTER AND OLIVE OIL

1 cup butter	4 egg yolks
1 teaspoon salt	1 tablespoon mustard
1 cup oil	¼ cup lemon juice
	¼ cup vinegar

Cream butter, stir smooth 4 egg yolks, vinegar, mustard, and salt. Add slowly oil, lemon juice and vinegar. Makes one quart of mayonnaise which may be mixed with whipped cream if desired. Does not separate. Keeps indefinitely.

MAYONNAISE DRESSING

1 egg	¾ cup olive or Wesson oil
1 small lemon	Salt and red pepper

Beat one egg yolk until thick, add juice of one small lemon. Add three-fourths cup oil slowly. Season with salt and pepper. Take care to beat thoroughly after adding salt until the salt is dissolved. If mayonnaise is not thick enough, add more oil very slowly. If mayonnaise curdles, take another egg yolk and add curdled mayonnaise to it, using the curdled mayonnaise as if it were oil.

MILLER AND RHOADS FRENCH DRESSING

1 quart oil	Salt, mustard and paprika to
¾ cup vinegar	taste
1 egg yolk	

Beat egg yolks with dry ingredients well. Add vinegar alternately with oil a little at a time, beating after each addition.

FRENCH DRESSING FOR FRUIT SALAD

1 cup oil	1 teaspoon salt
¼ cup vinegar	1 teaspoon dry mustard
½ cup powdered sugar	1 teaspoon paprika
1 teaspoon Worcestershire	1 grated clove
sauce	Juice of 1 lemon

Juice of 1 orange

Sauces

OYSTER CATSUP

Get fine fresh oysters, wash them in their own liquor, put them in a marble mortar with salt, pounded mace, and cayenne pepper, in the proportions of one ounce salt, two drachms mace, and one of cayenne to each pint of oysters; pound them together, and add a pint of white wine to each pint; boil it some minutes, and rub it through a sieve; boil it again, skim it, and when cold, bottle, cork, and seal it. This composition gives a fine flavor to white sauces, and if a glass of brandy be added, it will keep good for a considerable time.

"The Virginia Housewife"
by Mrs. Mary Randolph
Fourth Edition, Published 1830

HUNT CATSUP

One bushel tomatoes, firm and ripe. Wash, cut up in small pieces and cook thoroughly. Strain carefully. Cook the pulp for an hour and a half. Then add the following ingredients, for ten quarts of pulp:

8 onions that have been put through a food chopper

2 cups vinegar
3 pounds brown sugar

Salt to taste

Continue cooking until the mixture is thick, about an

hour and a half more. About twenty minutes before mixture is finished, add the following spices:

2 tablespoons ground cinnamon

1 tablespoon ground cloves

¼ teaspoon cayenne pepper

½ teaspoon nutmeg

Put into sterilized jars and seal at once.

This catsup will keep exceedingly well and is delicious served with cold meats as well as hot.

A SAUCE FOR MEATS

Melt together in a double boiler one glass of tart jelly (add a teaspoonful of lemon juice if jelly available is not tart), a generous tablespoon full of French mustard and two tablespoons of sherry. When blended add raisins which have been soaked a little while in hot water or slivers of citron.

Use hot on tongue, ham or roast pork.

"Ipsissima", Farmington

DELICIOUS FISH SAUCE

1 tablespoon butter
1 tablespoon flour
Juice of ½ lemon

1 tablespoon chopped parsley
1 pint consommé

Put the butter and flour in a sauce pan and let them blend without burning. Mix well over a slow fire and add consommé. Add the juice of lemon, chopped parsley and let all boil about 15 minutes. When it reaches this point, take off the stove, add the yolk of one egg, well-beaten. Mix well, stirring round and serve with boiled fish. Never add egg while sauce is on the fire as it will curdle immediately.

A SAUCE FOR FISH

½ stick of butter, or   1 teaspoon prepared mus-
  ⅛ pound   tard, the dark kind

Melt and brown butter very brown and stir in the mustard. Serve over sole or other fish.

COCKTAIL SAUCE

1 cup of mayonnaise   ½ teaspoon tabasco sauce
1 tablespoon tarragon vine- 1 cup chili sauce
  gar   ½ tablespoon anchovy paste

This is enough for one pint of shrimp. Use one-half portion for small can of crab meat.

SAUCE FOR OMELETTE

1 cup chopped onion   Few stuffed olives
1 can tomato soup   2 pieces chopped celery
              2 tablespoons green pepper

Broil one cup chopped onion in bacon fat until clear. Mix with tomato soup, green peppers and celery. Cook a while and season to taste. Add olives and pour on omelette just before serving.

"Wavertree Hall"

HOT SAUCE FOR AVOCADO

4 tablespoons butter   3 teaspoons sugar
2 tablespoons water   2 teaspoons Worcestershire
4 tablespoons ketchup   sauce
2 tablespoons vinegar   1/3 teaspoon salt
          Tabasco sauce, a dash

Mix the ingredients and cook for 20 minutes in double

boiler. Cut avocado in half, remove pit, and fill with *hot* sauce and serve with a watercress garnish for an appetizer.

FRENCH SAUCE FOR PUDDINGS

1 cup brown sugar
4 tablespoons butter
1 egg
Juice of 1 lemon

Thin slices of rind
1/3 cup wine, sherry or
   blackberry

Beat egg. Add sugar, butter and lemon. Simmer for 10 minutes. Add wine a short while before serving and a small amount of nutmeg grated. DO NOT BOIL after adding wine.

SAUCE FOR PLUM PUDDING

1 egg
¾ cup sugar
¾ cup heavy cream

Beat white of egg stiff. Add sugar gradually, beating constantly, then add yolk well-beaten. Add whipped cream, season with brandy.

SAUCE FOR PLUM PUDDING

1 pound brown sugar
½ pound butter
½ nutmeg
2 egg yolks
½ glass wine or whiskey

Cook sugar, butter, nutmeg in double boiler until smooth. Take from fire and add well-beaten eggs and wine or whiskey.

Hot Desserts

APPLE FRITTERS

Pare some apples, and cut them in thin slices—put them in a bowl, with a glass of brandy, some white wine, a quarter of a pound of pounded sugar, a little cinnamon finely powdered, and the rind of a lemon grated; let them stand some time, turning them over frequently; beat two eggs very light, add one quarter of a pound of flour, a tablespoonful of melted butter, and as much cold water as will make a thin batter; drip the apples on a sieve, mix them with the batter, take one slice with a spoonful of batter to each fritter, fry them quickly of a light brown, drain them well, put them in a dish, sprinkling sugar over each, and glaze them nicely.

"The Virginia Housewife"
by Mrs. Mary Randolph
Fourth Edition, Published 1830

APPLE CRUMBLE WITH NUTS

Peel and slice 6 to 8 medium apples and place in a shallow baking dish. Add ½ cup water, and if apples need additional tartness, add about 2 tablespoons lemon juice and a little grated rind. Season with 1 teaspoon cinnamon. Then mix ¾ cup flour, 1 cup brown sugar, ¼ cup butter, and 1/3 cup peanut butter. A pastry blender is good for this, or mix with the fingers. Sprinkle

the crumbly mixture over apples and bake in a moderate oven. Serve topped with whipped cream or ice cream.
Oven: 375° F. Time: 20 minutes. Serves: 6-8.

Note: ¼ cup more butter with ½ cup of thinly shaved almonds or chopped pecans may be substituted for the 1/3 cup peanut butter to vary this recipe.

BOILED PLUM PUDDING

¾ pound bread crumbs
¼ pound flour
½ pound butter
1 pound sugar
1 dozen eggs
2 pounds seeded raisins
2 pounds cleaned currants
½ pound citron
½ pound shelled almonds
1 teaspoon powdered nutmeg
1 teaspoon powdered cinnamon

1 teaspoon salt
2 teaspoons powdered allspice
1 teaspoon powdered cloves
1 teaspoon powdered mace
Grated rind and juice of 2 large oranges and 2 large lemons
2 gills of wine, or 1 each of wine and brandy, if procurable

Break and dry the bread for several days before the puddings are to be made. Grate it and sift the crumbs. Cream the butter and beat into it the sugar and spices carefully sifted. Beat egg yolks light and add to butter and sugar. Add the stiffly beaten whites and beat in lightly. Blanch the almonds, cut in half, split and dry thoroughly. Flour the fruit and almonds with a dust of the one-fourth pound of flour. Mix thoroughly all the dry ingredients, pour the egg mixture over them, add orange and lemon peel and juice, wine and brandy. Work with the hands until perfectly well-mixed. If very stiff, add one pint of cider or milk, if cider is not obtainable.　Butter pudding molds, fill with the mixture to within about two inches of the top, fasten the cover securely, and put into boiling water.　Boil until the pudding is firm and dry on top, from three to five hours, according to size of molds.　Boil them in a large closed vessel (meat roaster), water covering about two-thirds of the mold, and top shut tightly so the steam will cook the pudding.

This pudding takes several days in the making, but is worth the trouble.

"The Farm"

CRANBERRY PUDDING

One-half cup molasses.　Add two teaspoonfuls soda and at once fill cup to overflowing with hot water.

One and a half cups flour.　Mix the half cup of flour with one good cup raw cranberries.　Sift one teaspoonful baking powder with the remaining cup of flour.

Mix all together well and steam two to two and a half hours in covered well-greased mold.

Will serve six.

SAUCE

Melt in double boiler one-half cup butter.　Add one cup sugar and one-half cup cream.　Beat well and heat in double boiler.　Before serving, add one teaspoon vanilla.

DATE PUDDING

3 eggs well-beaten　　　　　　　1 cup sugar

Chop *coarsely* one-half pound of walnut meats and

one-half pound dates. Mix thoroughly the above and add the following:

1 tablespoon flour   Few drops of vanilla
          1 teaspoon baking powder

Bake in a slow oven for one-half hour. Serve with whipped cream.

MRS. RANDOLPH HARRISON'S FIG PUDDING

2 cups stale bread crumbs   3 eggs well beaten
1 cup chopped stewed figs   1 teaspoon cinnamon
½ cup butter   1 wine glass sherry wine
1 cup sugar   1 cup chopped pecans

Use enough juice from figs to moisten mixture well. Put into covered vessel and steam three hours. Serve with hard sauce.

"Tall Pines"

GEORGIA PUDDING

6 eggs   2 cups sugar
5 tablespoons hot, mashed   1 cup currants
  Irish potatoes   1 cup raisins
2 heaping tablespoons butter   1 teaspoon ground cinnamon

Mix butter and sugar, then eggs, then stir in other ingredients.

Bake in greased baking dish at 350° F. for about three-quarters of an hour and serve with wine sauce.

MACAROON PUDDING

2 dozen macaroons   ½ cup cream
6 eggs   ½ cup sugar
          Blanched almonds

Beat yolks and sugar together. Add one-half cup

cream and sherry. Put into double boiler and cook until it thickens into a custard. Pour over broken macaroons laid in a baking dish. Whip whites of eggs and to white of each egg, add one tablespoon of sugar. Pour the sweetened, whipped white of eggs over custard and macaroons and brown in oven. Stick top thickly with blanched almonds and serve hot. *"Wavertree Hall"*

CREAM RICE PUDDING

1 quart fresh milk
3 level tablespoons of well-washed rice
1 pinch salt
¾ tablespoon of granulated sugar
Grated nutmeg to taste

Mix all ingredients together and bake in earthenware dish slowly for two hours in moderate oven, stirring the first half hour. Secret of creamy pudding is in the slow baking.

Serves: 6.

SWEET POTATO PUDDING

An old family recipe from Georgia.

2 cups grated raw sweet potato
⅞ cup brown sugar
2 eggs
2 tablespoons molasses
½ teaspoon salt
¼ cup melted butter
1 teaspoon ginger
⅛ teaspoon cinnamon
⅛ teaspoon nutmeg
½ cup milk

Grate potatoes fine. Beat eggs. Add sugar, then molasses, butter, spices and milk. Beat well and bake in well-greased casserole at 350° F. until firm, or about one hour. *"Kinloch"*

Serves 6-8.

WOODFORD PUDDING

1 cup sugar	1 cup flour
3 eggs	3 teaspoons sour milk
½ cup butter	1 teaspoon soda
½ cup jam	Cinnamon to taste

Cream sugar and butter. Add eggs beaten separately. Add flour, jam and milk, first dissolving soda in the milk. Add cinnamon. Beat all together thoroughly and bake in slow oven in cake tin or pyrex dish.

SAUCE FOR PUDDING

2 eggs, whites only	Vanilla to taste
1 tablespoon vinegar	½ cup rich cream
1 cup sugar	3 tablespoons wine

Beat whites of eggs until stiff. Add sugar, vinegar, vanilla, and wine and just before serving, add the cream, stirring in thoroughly.

"Credenhill"

CARAMEL SOUFFLE

2/3 cup sugar for caramelizing	¾ cup milk
2 tablespoons butter	2 tablespoons sugar
2 tablespoons flour	¾ teaspoon vanilla
2 eggs	Salt
	½ pint heavy cream

Caramelize the sugar to light brown, pour into glass pie plate and tip it until well-coated. Melt the butter, add flour and milk, stir until thick. Remove from fire, add salt and yolks of 2 eggs. Beat well, cool slightly. Add sugar and vanilla. Fold in stiffly beaten egg whites. Turn into caramelized dish. Set in a pan of water and bake in a slow oven 35-40 minutes.

Whip the cream until stiff. Sweeten slightly and add a few drops of vanilla. Run knife around edge of souffle and move to a heated round platter. Put whipped cream on top. Caramel syrup and cream will form a sauce.

MARTHA GLENNON'S HOT CHERRY SOUFFLE

Top Mixture

1 tablespoon butter	3 eggs, separated
1 tablespoon flour	¼ cup sugar
2/3 cup warm milk	1 dessert spoon liquor

Bottom Mixture

1 can black Bing cherries, pitted	½ teaspoon corn starch
	½ lemon rind, grated
¼ cup sugar, mixed with	2 tablespoons liquor

Melt butter in double boiler, add flour, stir and cook a few minutes. Add milk. Stir smoothly and well and cook until creamy. Cool. Add well-beaten egg yolks to which sugar has been added, then liquor. Put aside.

Strain juice off cherries. Thoroughly cook juice to which the corn starch has been added. When syrupy, add cherries that have been soaked in liquor and lemon rind. Butter and sugar casserole dish. Put in cherries and juice.

Then take first mixture and add well-beaten egg whites to which add 1 tablespoon of sugar. Fold all gently and put on top of cherry mixture.

Bake 25 to 30 minutes in casserole set in pan of water at 350° F. oven temperature. Serve with whipped cream if you like.

DATE SOUFFLE

1½ cups milk
1/3 cup flour
2 tablespoons butter

1/3 cup sugar
1 cup dates
3 eggs

1 teaspoon vanilla

Cook the milk, flour and butter in double boiler until thick and smooth. Then add sugar, dates ground through a meat chopper, and egg yolks with whites beaten stiff, and vanilla. Set in a pan of water and bake in a slow oven. Serve wtih whipped cream, not sweetened.

CREME BRULE

2 cups XX cream
½ inch of vanilla bean
(vanilla extract)

4 egg yolks
1 cup granulated sugar

Heat cream over slow fire with vanilla bean. Beat yolks with 4 tablespoons sugar until creamy and light. Mix in warm cream slowly and carefully. Return to thick pan and place on slow fire and stir constantly until the mixture coats the back of a wooden spoon. Pour into a shallow glass dish and chill *overnight* in refrigerator. Next day, cover the top completely with the sugar so that no cream shows. Place on top of a bowl of crushed ice and place under broiler with high flame until the sugar caramelizes. Chill 3 minutes and serve.

CREPES SUZETTE

½ cup flour
3 tablespoons powdered sugar

1 egg
¼ teaspoon salt
½ cup milk

Mix dry ingredients, add milk, stir until quite smooth.

Add egg, beat thoroughly. Add grated rind of one lemon to mixture at last moment. Cook as ordinary pancakes. Roll and serve with the following sauce:

6 tablespoons butter	Grated rind and juice of 2
1 cup powdered sugar	oranges

Cream the butter. Beat in sugar gradually. Add the rind and juice and last, two tablespoons of curaçao and one of brandy.   *"Bloomfield"*

BREAD PUDDING WITH DAMSON PRESERVES

2 cups stale bread crumbs	1 quart milk
1½ cups sugar	Pinch of salt
Yolks of 5 eggs, slightly beaten	½ teaspoon vanilla

Meringue: ½ cup of sugar and the whites of 5 eggs. Soak bread crumbs in milk. Add other ingredients and pour into buttered baking dish. Bake about an hour in a moderate oven. When it has cooled, spread top of pudding with damson preserves to desired thickness. Beat whites of eggs until stiff, then add sugar gradually, continuing to beat. Cover pudding with this meringue and run into the oven for a few seconds to brown on top.

AN OLD RECIPE FOR GINGERBREAD

¾ cup butter	1 teaspoon ginger
1 cup sugar	1 teaspoon cinnamon
3 cups flour	½ teaspoon cloves
1 cup dark molasses	1 teaspoon soda
1 cup black coffee	3 eggs

1 teaspoon baking powder added to flour

Mix spices with molasses. Dissolve soda in a little hot

water and add to the coffee. Cream together butter and sugar. Add eggs, one at a time, beating well after each addition. Add molasses, then the coffee and flour, a little at a time alternately. Bake in two square cake pans, in moderate oven for 40-60 minutes, or until cake leaves side of pan.

PEACH COBBLER

To:

4 cups sliced fresh peaches,   1½ cups sugar
  add

Bake closely covered until peaches are tender.

Cream:

2 tablespoons butter with   1 cup flour that has been
¼ cup sugar. Beat in   sifted with
1 egg   ¼ teaspoon salt and
½ cup milk, and   1 teaspoon baking powder.

Pour over hot fruit and bake 25 minutes at 400° F. Serve with hard sauce.

PEACH UPSIDE-DOWN CAKE

1 can peaches   1 cup brown sugar
½ cup butter   Pinch salt
                    Dash nutmeg

Cream butter and sugar together, add salt and nutmeg, and spread on bottom of a pyrex cake sheet. Place peach halves, hollow side up, on mixture, and cover with rich cake batter. Bake in a moderate oven at 375° F. for 25-30 minutes. When slightly cooled, remove from cake pan, turn upside down, and serve with whipped cream or vanilla ice cream.

Cold Desserts

CANTON CREAM

Soak 1 tablespoon granulated gelatin in ¼ cup cold water. Add custard made of 1 cup milk, yolks of 2 eggs, ¼ cup sugar and a few grains salt. Strain, chill in pan of ice water, add 1 tablespoon ginger syrup and ¼ cup Canton ginger cut into small pieces. When mixture begins to thicken fold in whip from 2½ cups cream. Mold and chill.

"Tall Pines"

CHARLOTTE RUSSE

1 pint whipped cream
1 tablespoon gelatin soaked in ¼ cup of milk

3 tablespoons sugar
Whites of 4 eggs beaten stiff
1 teaspoon vanilla

Whip sugar into whites of eggs. Add to whipped cream. Season with vanilla. Stir gelatin into mixture and pour into molds lined with lady fingers or sponge cake.

CHARLOTTE RUSSE

Beat together well two egg yolks and add three table-spoons of granulated sugar. Put one-half cup milk in double boiler to scald. Pour over yolks and sugar, and stir over low flame until it coats the spoon.

Add to this hot custard, one tablespoon of gelatin which has been soaked for a half hour in four tablespoons of water. Stir until dissolved. Then add flavoring, either vanilla or sherry to taste, then the well-beaten whites of two eggs. Beat until it begins to thicken. Then mix in lightly, one pint of cream which has been whipped to a stiff froth, and turn into a mold lined with lady fingers.

ANGEL CHARLOTTE RUSSE

1 envelope Knox gelatin	1 dozen marshmallows
½ dozen rolled stale maca-	2 tablespoons cherries
roons	¼ pound blanched almonds
1 cup sugar	¼ cup cold water
1 pint heavy cream	¼ cup boiling water

Vanilla to taste

Soak gelatin in cold water five minutes, then dissolve in boiling water and add sugar.

When mixture is cold, add cream well-beaten, or beat this mixture into the well-beaten cream. Then add macaroons crumbled, almonds ground, marshmallows cut up, and cherries cut up. Stir all well. Put in wet mold and chill. Serve with whipped cream.

"Gallison Hall"

ANGEL TIPSY PUDDING

Split whole angel cake into 2 layers. On bottom layer drip enough sherry to give a good flavoring and spread with layer of rather stiff cold custard sauce flavored with sherry. Then sprinkle with blanched almonds. Top with second layer also sprinkled with sherry. Ice the whole cake with whipped cream. Add more blanched, split almonds. Ararnge on large plate and slice like layer cake, serving with it more custard sauce in a side pitcher.

RUM CAKE

1 large, light sponge cake   2 cups rum syrup
2 cups or more of cream filling

SYRUP

¾ cup rum   ¾ cup water
½ cup sugar

Bring to a boil and simmer a couple of minutes.

CREAM FILLING

Scald 2 cups milk with grated lemon rind. Add 2 tablespoons cornstarch and ½ cup sugar. When thick, add 2 or 3 egg yolks and cook for 3 minutes more. Cool and flavor with rum to taste.

Now split your cake in 3 layers. Sprinkle generously with rum syrup each side of the layers. Spread your filling and be sure to have it soft enough to soak in a bit, but not run off at the sides. Have a good *thick* layer of the filling between each slice. Ice cake with a 7 minute frosting flavored with rum, or better still, with a butter frosting sprinkled with toasted, sugared almond crumbs. The cake is best prepared 24 hours ahead, so the cream filling soaks in.

SHERRY PUDDING

6 egg yolks   1 pint whipping cream
2 cups sugar   1 teaspoon vanilla
2 cups sherry   2 packages Knox gelatin

Soak gelatin until dissolved. Whip yolks, sugar and cream together. Add sherry, vanilla and gelatin. Put in mold, then in ice box. Garnish with jelly.

"Cismont Manor"

TEXAS EGGNOG RING

4 eggs
½ cup sugar
1 tablespoon gelatin soaked
   in ¼ cup cold water
¼ cup boiling water

½ cup whiskey
1 teaspoon vanilla
1 pint whipping cream
1/3 cup ground almonds
4 crushed macaroons

Separate eggs and beat whites until very stiff. Dissolve gelatin in boiling water and pour over whites. Put whiskey and vanilla in well-beaten yolks, to which sugar has been added, and add to whites. When mixture begins to congeal, put in ring mold and leave until set.

Turn out and fill center with mixture of whipped cream, almonds and macaroons.

CHOCOLATE SUNSHINE

Soak 1 tablespoon gelatin in ½ cup cold water. Melt 2 squares chocolate in top of double boiler. Stir until smooth. Add 3 well-beaten egg yolks into which ½ cup sugar has been stirred. Blend with chocolate and beat hard, still over hot water, until mixture thickens. Add ¼ teaspoon cinnamon. Remove from fire and add gelatin. Let cool while you beat 4 egg whites until stiff.

With as light a hand as possible, gradually fold chocolate mixture into egg whites. *Don't beat.*

Pour into bowl in which it is to be served. Set in ice box one hour or more . Serve with whipped cream.

Serves 5.

ITALIAN CHESTNUT TORTA

Shell a pound of chestnuts, cook, remove skins, and rub through strainer. Add the weight of chestnuts in eggs and one-half weight in sugar. Mix yolks, sugar, and chestnuts together. Add one teaspoon of vanilla and a lemon peel. Add the whites beaten stiff. Put in form, bake about one-half hour. Let cool, and serve with whipped cream.

MONT BLANC

3 cups French chestnuts shelled	Hot milk
	Vanilla
Powdered sugar	Whipped cream

Cook chestnuts in a little boiling water. When they are soft and the water is boiled away, mash them and sweeten with powdered sugar to taste, and moisten with hot milk. Cook this mixture for two minutes. Rub through a strainer, cool, and flavor with vanilla or wine. Pile in a pyramid and cover with whipped cream.

COFFEE ICE BOX CAKE

1 pound marshmallows	1½ pints whipped cream
1 cup chopped almonds	4 dozen lady fingers
2 cups strong black coffee	

Put coffee and marshmallows in double boiler and stir until marshmallows are dissolved. Let cool. Then add nuts and whipped cream. Make layers of split lady fingers in ice tray lined with wax paper and pour cooled mixture over split lady fingers. Place in ice box until hard, or about 2½ hours. Turn out and cover with whipped cream. Decorate with canned cherries and almonds, as desired.

Serves 8.

DATE ROLL

1 pound dates	12 graham crackers—take
1 pound pecans	3 out
1 pound marshmallows	1 cup milk

Chop dates and nuts. Cut marshmallows with wet scissors. Roll crackers. Mix and make into a roll. Coat outside with the three crackers rolled fine. Wrap in oil paper and let stand. Slice and serve with whipped cream.

"Hathaway"

RASPBERRY ICE BOX DESSERT

1½ packages of raspberry gelatin	24 lady fingers
	2 eggs
1 can raspberries	1 pint double cream
20 marshmallows	

Strain berries and add water enough to make 2 cups of juice. Boil and pour over gelatin. When cool, whip until light, add beaten eggs, purée of berries, and one-half the cream whipped.

Line 2 bread pans with waxed paper so cake can be lifted out with split lady fingers. Pour in the mixture and put in the ice box for 12 hours. If wanted sweeter, add sugar and serve with whipped cream.

STRAWBERRY ICE BOX DESSERT

1 pound vanilla wafers	2 eggs
¼ pound butter	1 quart strawberries, cut up
1½ cups XXXX sugar	½ pint whipping cream

Crush wafers fine and put more than one-half in the bottom of a pan 8 x 12 x 2. Cream butter and sugar. Add eggs one at a time and beat well. Flavor with vanilla and add a little cream if necessary. Spread over the crumbs in the pan and cover with sliced strawberries, or strained defrosted frozen berries, and sprinkle with sugar. Spread over with flavored whipped cream and cover with remaining crumbs. Place in refrigerator and let remain overnight or at least for several hours before serving.

CHOCOLATE ROLL

5 egg yolks	5 tablespoons sugar
5 egg whites	1 tablespoon potato flour, or
5 tablespoons cocoa	cake flour
1 teaspoon vanilla	

Line a jelly cake pan, or cookie sheet, with waxed paper, buttered. Beat whites stiff. Add cocoa, sugar and vanilla. Last, add the beaten yolks. Bake 20 minutes in a slow oven. Turn out on a damp cloth. Cut crusts from edges, and roll cake and towel together. When cool, carefully unroll, remove towel, place cake on waxed paper, and cover with whipped cream beaten very stiff, flavored with vanilla and powdered sugar. Roll carefully again, using wax paper as a help in rolling. Place on serving plate with edge down to keep roll in place. This should not stand very long before serving, although one-half an hour or so in the refrigerator does not harm it. It should not become soggy, and cream must be whipped dry. The following sauce makes it especially good for dessert:

1 square chocolate	1 cup sugar
1 tablespoon melted butter	1 teaspoon vanilla
1/3 cup boiling water	1 teaspoon brandy flavoring

Melt chocolate in double boiler. Add the butter, blend thoroughly, and pour on gradually the boiling water, stirring constantly. Then add the sugar. Bring to the boiling point and cook 15 minutes without stirring. Cool and add flavoring. Keep warm in double boiler until served. The ingredients must be added in sequence to insure a smooth sauce.

CHOCOLATE PEPPERMINT ROLL

1/3 cup flour	4 egg whites
1/3 cup cocoa	1 cup sugar
1 teaspoon baking powder	4 egg yolks
¼ teaspoon salt	2 tablespoons water

1 teaspoon vanilla extract

Mix flour, cocoa, baking powder and salt together. Beat egg whites until they point, but not until dry. Fold in one-half the sugar. Add water to egg yolks; beat until light; add remaining sugar gradually; beat until fluffy. Fold into beaten whites. Fold in sifted dry ingredients; add vanilla extract.

Pour into shallow pan lined with heavy waxed paper; bake in moderate oven.

When baked, turn out cake on paper or cloth sprinkled with powdered sugar. Remove waxed paper; trim off edges of cake. Roll up cake at once in the cloth or paper. When cool, unroll and spread with Peppermint Filling. Roll up again and store in refrigerator. Cut in slices to serve.

Temperature: 400°F. Time: 15-20 minutes.

PEPPERMINT FILLING

½ cup crushed peppermint cream patties—or ⅛ teaspoon peppermint extract and ¼ cup sugar
1 cup cream, whipped

Peppermint cream patties should have a creamy center

and be soft enough to crush with a fork. Fold crushed patties or peppermint extract and sugar, into whipped cream.

PERSIMMON PUDDING

As Made in Carolina

One-half gallon persimmons, capped, mashed, and thinned in 1½ pints water. Strain through cheese cloth bag.

Add to the batter:

3 cups sifted flour
1¼ cups sugar
1 grated sweet potato, size of a pint cup
1 tablespoon butter
3 eggs, well-beaten

2 cups milk, sweet or sour
½ teaspoon soda for sweet milk, or 2 level teaspoons if sour milk is used
1 level teaspoon salt

Flavor with vanilla and grated nutmeg. Bake in very slow oven until brown and well set, or from 1½ to 2 hours. Cut in squares and serve topped with whipped cream and nuts.

This will keep in the ice chest for two weeks and is better as it ages.

BLACK CHERRY RING

1 can black Bing cherries   1 package cherry jello
Juice from the cherries and enough sherry wine to make
2 cups liquid in all

Dissolve jello in ½ cherry juice which has been heated. Add to this the remainder of juice and the sherry with the cherries, and pour into a ring mold to chill thoroughly. When ready to serve unmold and fill center with whipped cream sweetened to taste.

WINE JELLY

2 envelopes gelatin	1 cup sugar
1 cup cold water	½ cup lemon juice
1¼ cups boiling water	¾ cup sherry or port

Soak gelatin in cold water for five minutes. Dissolve in boiling water. Add sugar and stir until completely dissolved. Next, add lemon juice and sherry or port. Pour into a mold to chill. Serve with whipped cream. This makes 1 quart.

Ice Cream and Ices

FROZEN PUDDING

1 pint milk	½ scant cup flour or corn-starch
1 quart cream	
2 eggs	½ pound or more candied fruit
2 cups granulated sugar	
2 tablespoons gelatin soaked in a little water	4 tablespoons sherry wine

Let milk come to a boil. Beat eggs, flour, and one cup of sugar together and put in boiling milk. Cook twenty minutes. Add gelatin and set away to cool. When cool, add cream, wine, and sugar. Freeze for short while, then add fruit and continue to freeze. Pack for an hour or two to ripen.

FROZEN APPLE FLOAT

Take six medium apples, pare, core and cut up. Stew slowly with as little water as possible and cook until clear and stiff, not watery. Press through colander, sweeten to taste, and flavor with lemon extract if apples are flavorless. Add stiffly beaten whites of two eggs and one-half pint whipped cream sweetened. Pack in ice and salt, or particularly good in electric refrigerator.

Serves 8.

BLACKBERRY ICE CREAM

1 quart cream	1 quart milk
2 tablespoons flour	3 teacups of sugar
1 quart blackberries	

Scald milk in a double boiler. Then mix flour thoroughly in two cups of sugar and stir into the scalded milk. Let this cook fifteen minutes, stirring all the time to keep from lumping. Take from the fire and strain it and set aside to cool. Wash berries well. Cover with one cup of sugar, let stand a little while, and then mash and strain. When scalded milk is cool, stir in cream and strained juice of berries and freeze.

"Woodville"

ICE CREAM AND STRAWBERRIES

1 quart strawberries. Wash and hull. Mash strawberries through sieve. Add juice of ½ lemon, and enough sugar to sweeten, rather sweet. Freeze in refrigerator tray. Then put either sweetened whipped cream or 1 quart of vanilla ice cream on top. Continue at freezing temperature until ready to serve. Cut in squares and turn out.

Serves about 8.

MOCK PISTACHIO ICE CREAM

1¼ cups top milk	1 cup whipping cream
1½ tablespoons flour	2 egg whites
½ cup sugar	1½ teaspoons vanilla
2 egg yolks	1 teaspoon almond extract
Green coloring	Pinch salt

Mix flour and sugar thoroughly. Add cold milk and stir to a smooth paste. Stir constantly over direct heat until thick, then cook over hot water for ten minutes. Remove, add well-beaten egg yolks and cook over hot water two minutes. Strain and cool. Add flavoring, coloring, well-beaten egg whites, and whipped cream. Freeze. Beat once in bowl with rotary beater when frozen for about one inch from edge of pan.

Serves 6.

"Meadow Creek Farm"

Note: This is good served in meringues.

LEMON SHERBET

1½ cups sugar
2 cups boiling water
2 lemons, juice; and rind of
   one grated

¼ teaspoon salt
2 egg yolks
2 cups cream, whipped
2 egg whites, beaten stiff

Dissolve sugar in boiling water, add grated rind and juice of fruit, then salt. Pour gradually over well-beaten egg yolks, then cool and freeze to a mushy consistency in refrigerator tray. Beat until stiff and add a little sugar.

Beat whites until stiff, then fold cream and egg whites into the half-frozen mixture and continue freezing. Stir two or three times during freezing.

"Retreat"

RASPBERRY ICE

1 quart raspberries

1 cup sugar sprinkled over
   berries

Let stand two to three hours, then drip overnight.

In the morning, add 2 tablespoons lemon juice and ½ cup water to every quart of fruit juice. Three quarts fruit makes 1 quart of juice.

Freeze according to Boston Cooking School Book.

"Cismont Manor"

FROZEN ORANGE MAPLE

One egg and one orange to each person.

Separate eggs, add juice of oranges to beaten yolks, and sweeten to taste with maple syrup. Add well-beaten whites and to every eight eggs, add one cup of cream. Freeze very hard. Serve in sherbet glasses with plain cake, preferably sponge cake. Very rich, so small serving is sufficient.

ALMOND PARFAIT

¼ pound shelled almonds   1 quart cream
                1 cup sugar

Blanch almonds and chop fine. Brown sugar on top of stove, add almonds and continue browning, stirring all the time. Put mixture into greased pan to cool. When cool, put through meat grinder and add to the cream, beaten stiff and sweetened. Put into mold, pack in ice and salt, and let stand for 3 hours.

MACAROON PARFAIT

½ cup sugar   ¼ cup water
3 egg yolks   ¼ pound crushed macaroons
1 teaspoon vanilla   1 pint cream

Put water and sugar on to boil and cook until mixture spins a thread. Beat egg yolks to a cream. Add to boiling syrup and beat over a fire to a custard. Strain through sieve into bowl and beat until stiff and cold. Add macaroons, vanilla and cream. Stir these carefully into mixture. Put in mold and pack in ice and salt for 3 hours.

Pies and Pastries

APPLE DUMPLINGS

2 cups sugar	6 apples
2 cups water	2 cups enriched flour
¼ teaspoon cinnamon	1 teaspoon salt
¼ teaspoon nutmeg	2 teaspoons baking powder
¼ cup butter	¾ cup shortening

½ cup milk

Sauce: Cook sugar, water and spices 5 minutes. Add butter. Pare and core apples.

Pastry: Sift flour, salt, and baking powder. Cut in shortening. Add milk all at once and stir just until flour is moistened. Roll ¼ inch thick. Cut into 6 squares. Place apple on each, sprinkle with added sugar and spices, dot with butter, fold and pinch edges. Place 1 inch apart in greased baking dish. Pour over sauce and bake in moderate oven at 375° F. for 35 minutes. Serve hot with heavy cream.

BLACKBERRY ROLL

Make a good pastry and roll it out on the biscuit board. Then sprinkle the pastry thick with berries that have been washed and drained. Next, sprinkle with sugar and a little butter. Roll up, and put in a buttered dish to bake slowly until done, about three-quarters of an hour. Serve hot with hard sauce.

Hard Sauce: Mix well 1 cup of butter with 1 cup brown sugar and 1 cup powdered sugar, add the juice of one-half a lemon. Put this in the dish in which it is to be served and sprinkle with grated nutmeg. Then put it in the refrigerator until just before serving.

"Cloverfields"

BUTTER SCOTCH PIE

1½ cups milk	2 tablespoons cornstarch
1½ cups dark brown sugar	Butter, size of an egg

3 eggs, separated

Put milk on to heat and put in cornstarch. Cook until thick. Beat eggs and sugar together. Add to milk and cook until thick. Cool before pouring in crust. Make meringue from beaten whites with one tablespoon sugar to each egg.

CHEESE CAKE PIE

Prepare a Zwieback crust or Graham cracker crust.

Filling

2 cups cottage cheese	3 tablespoons lemon juice
1 cup granulated sugar	1 tablespoon grated orange
¼ teaspoon salt	rind
½ teaspoon baking powder	3 eggs, beaten
3 tablespoons butter, melted	2 tablespoons rice flour

Mix cheese, sugar, flour, salt, baking powder, and melted butter. Blend well. Add lemon juice and grated rind and slightly beaten eggs. Beat whole mixture with rotary egg beater for 2 minutes. Pour into unbaked shell. Bake 10 minutes in moderately hot oven of 400° F. Lower heat to moderately slow oven of 300° F. and bake further 30 minutes. Serve cold with whipped cream if desired.

Oven 1st: 400° F.—10 minutes; 300° F.—30 minutes. Serves 6.

CHESS CAKES

Yolks of 12 eggs	½ pound butter
Whites of 2 eggs	2 tablespoons corn meal
1 pound sugar	Juice of 2 lemons

Cream butter and sugar together. Add well-beaten eggs, then corn meal and lemon juice. Bake in muffin tins lined with pastry. This makes twenty.

ROSA'S CHESS PIE

½ cup butter	3 egg yolks
½ cup sugar	½ teaspoon vanilla

Cream butter and sugar together, and add slightly beaten egg yolks and vanilla. Pour into uncooked pastry shell and cook in a slow oven until set. Make meringue with egg whites.

The Lawn

CHOCOLATE PIE

3 egg yolks	2 tablespoons chocolate,
1 cup sugar	melted
1 tablespoon flour	1 cup boiling water

Mix ingredients evenly and add water slowly. Cook in double boiler and add vanilla. Fill baked pie crust. Make a meringue of stiffly beaten whites.

"Cloverfields"

CREAM PIE

7 eggs
1 pint granulated sugar
½ cup of thick cream

½ cup butter
1 tablespoon lemon juice
6 tablespoons of sugar

Mix yolks of eggs and white of one egg, sugar, cream, butter, and lemon juice. Bake in pie crust. Do not have oven too hot. Beat whites of six eggs to stiff froth and add six tablespoons sugar, one spoon at a time. Beat well and put on top of pie when it is done. Brown in oven.

CARAMEL PIE

MADE WITH DAMSON PRESERVES

4 eggs, beaten separately
1 cup cream
1 cup damson preserves, seeded

1 cup sugar
1 cup butter
2 teaspoons vanilla

Cream butter and sugar. Add yolks of eggs, preserves, cream and vanilla, then whites of eggs. Pour into pastry and bake uncovered. This makes four pies.

"Gale Hill"

LEMON PIE

1 tablespoon butter
1 tablespoon Crisco

2 cups sugar
4 eggs

Juice of 3 lemons

Cream butter and Crisco. Add sugar, eggs which have been lightly beaten, and lemon juice. Pour into un-cooked pie crust and bake at 325° F. oven temperature until crust is done and pie filling is set. Chill. Serve with whipped cream if desired.

LEMON PIE

4 eggs   ⅛ teaspoon salt
1 cup sugar   3 tablespoons water
                1 lemon, juice and rind

Cook yolks of eggs, one-half cup of sugar, salt, lemon juice and grated rind and water in double boiler until thick, five or ten minutes stirring constantly. Remove from fire and stir into whites beaten stiff with rest of sugar. Put in baked shell and bake in hot oven 375° F. to 400° F. until nicely browned.

LEMON AND COCOANUT PIES

LEMON

Use 10 yolks and 2 whites of eggs beaten until light, with pinch of salt. Add sugar, ½ pound gradually, and juice and grated rind of 1 lemon. Then ¼ pound of butter, creamed, and put into 2 small pastry pie crusts and bake slowly.

COCOANUT

Beat whites of 8 eggs with pinch of salt until very light. Add ½ pound sugar gradually, 1½ pounds creamed butter and a grated cocoanut. Stir in lightly vanilla, a little rose water, sherry or brandy. Put into 2 pastry shells and bake slowly. Use very rich pastry.

ORANGE PIE

3 eggs   1 tablespoon butter, melted
1 cup cream   Grated rind and juice of 2
1 cup sugar   oranges
1 tablespoon flour

Beat the eggs and sugar well together, sprinkle flour

into it and beat smooth. Add grated rind and juice of the oranges, cream, and melted butter. Pour into pastry and bake. *"Cloverfields"*

MRS. FITZHUGH LEE'S MINCE MEAT

2 pounds beef	1½ pounds lemon peel
2 pounds currants	4 pounds apples
2 pounds raisins	2 pounds sultana raisins
1 pound citron	2 pounds sugar
2 pounds suet	2 grated nutmegs
¼ ounce cinnamon	1 teaspoon salt
¼ ounce cloves	2 lemons, juice and rind

2 oranges, juice and rind

Simmer meat until tender. When perfectly cold, chop it fine, seed the rasins, shred the citron, pare, core, and peel the apples. Mix the dry ingredients, then add the juice of the oranges and lemons. Pack in jars, cover well and keep cool. This will keep all winter. This rule is an old one and was used in the Custis family. The Widow Custis, who became Mrs. Washington, made famous mince pies.

MINCE MEAT

2 pounds lean beef, boiled and cut fine	2½ pounds brown sugar
	1 quart brown sherry
1 pound suet, chopped raw	1 pint whiskey
5 pounds apples, chopped	2 tablespoons cinnamon
2 pounds raisins	1 tablespoon mace
2 pounds currants	1 tablespoon cloves
½ pound citron	1 tablespoon allspice
1 pound sultana raisins	1 tablespoon salt

Add orange juice or strong lemonade to each pie, as baked, and a little brandy.

This makes about 16 pies. *"Spring Hill"*

PECAN PIE

2 cups pecans, whole
2 cups corn syrup
2½ tablespoons butter

4 eggs
2 cups sugar
2¼ tablespoons vanilla

Cream butter and sugar. Add syrup, beaten eggs, pecans and vanilla. Beat well.

Put mixture in unbaked pie shells and cook very slowly at 275° F. oven temperature for 30 minutes. Serve with whipped cream.

PECAN PIE

3 eggs
½ teaspoon salt
1 teaspoon vanilla

1 tablespoon melted butter
1 cup sugar
1 cup thin cream

1½ cups pecans

Whip eggs together and add other ingredients. Pour into unbaked pastry shell. Cook until custard is set.

"Cloverfields"

ZWIEBACK TORTE

1 teaspoon cinnamon
¼ cup sugar
½ cup melted butter

1 package Zweiback rolled to fine crumbs

Mix above ingredients together and fill bottom and sides of spring pan with mixture. Put in oven and brown slightly. Save enough of the mixture to sprinkle over the top to make a thin crust.

Cook in a double boiler:

½ cup sugar
Yolks of 3 eggs
1 teaspoon vanilla

1 heaping tablespoon corn-starch
2 cups scalded milk

Put this cooked custard in the browned shell. Beat

3 egg whites with ½ cup sugar and a little vanilla to make meringue. Spread the meringue over the custard, cover with the rest of the crumbs and bake in moderate oven for 20 minutes. Serve cold.

Oven: 350° F. Time: 20 minutes. Serves: 6.

TEA TARTS

1 stick butter, or ¼ pound   1 package cream cheese
1 cup flour

Allow butter and cream cheese to soften. When soft, combine, then work in flour. Place in refrigerator to chill. When thoroughly chilled, remove and roll out for cutting, using a round 3-inch cutter. Put orange marmalade, preserves, or jelly in center, and fold over, pressing edges together lightly. Bake in moderate oven 10-12 minutes.

SCOTCH SHORTBREAD

1 pound flour   ¼ pound sugar
½ pound butter

Cream butter and sugar, not too creamy. Mix in the flour slowly with a wooden spoon. When mixture becomes too stiff to work in basin, turn onto well-floured board and knead in the remainder of the flour. Divide dough into three parts and knead each part into an oblong cake. Roll each, and mark with a fork. Bake in a moderate oven until brown. While still hot, sprinkle with sugar and cut into fingers.

"Cotswold"

Cakes

BISCUIT DE SAVOIE

3 eggs
½ cup sugar

¾ cup flour, sifted before
measuring

Vanilla

Separate eggs. Beat yolks, sugar, and vanilla together. Add flour, and then whites beaten stiff. Pour in buttered and floured tin. Bake 30 minutes in moderate oven. When cold, slice very thin into three layers and frost with the following:

2½ tablespoons very strong
coffee

2½ tablespoons sugar
1 egg yolk

3 tablespoons butter

Boil until thick the sugar and water. Beat egg yolk and add syrup drop by drop. Beat until cool. Add butter in small pieces, piece by piece. Beat until smooth. When enough butter has been added this frosting will stand alone and hold its shape. Add more butter if necessary. Spread on cake when both are cool.

This will taste and look better if sprinkled with chopped nuts or rock sugar, or if frosting is topped with rosettes made of frosting with a pastry tube. For chocolate frosting, use one tablespoon of cocoa and two tablespoons of water instead of the coffee.

WALNUT CAKE

1 cup milk	¾ cup butter
2 cups sugar	3 cups flour
3 even teaspoons of baking powder	3 eggs

Not quite a cup full of broken English walnut meats.

Beat butter and sugar together and add milk slowly. Beat separately the yolks and whites of eggs. Add baking powder to flour. Mix all together, adding nut meats last.

Bake in square pans, ice with boiled icing. Put one-half walnut meats at intervals, so that cakes can be cut into squares.

BOILED ICING

3 cups sugar	3 egg whites beaten until
1 cup water	very stiff

Boil sugar and water until the syrup threads when poured from spoon. Add to whites beating constantly until the proper consistency to spread. Season with vanilla.

MRS. CHALFIN'S CARAWAY CAKE

1 cup butter	¾ cup milk
3 cups flour	Yolks of 5 eggs
1½ cups powdered sugar	Whites of 2 eggs, unbeaten
¼ teaspoon salt	1 teaspoon vanilla
2½ teaspoons baking powder	½ teaspoon almond flavoring

2 to 4 teaspoons caraway seeds, according to taste

Cream butter until very soft. Add sugar slowly, stirring well. Add yolks one at a time. Sift dry ingredients, adding alternately with the milk. Stir in whites of eggs and beat well. Add the flavorings and caraway seeds. Two teaspoons of caraway seeds give a nice flavor. Four teaspoons are for those who are very fond of them.

Bake in a greased and floured small tube pan for about one hour, using a moderate oven. This is similar to pound cake, but not quite so rich.

COCOANUT CAKE

2 cups sugar	1 cup fresh cocoanut milk
½ cup butter	4 egg whites
3 cups cake flour	4 teaspoons baking powder

Cream butter and add sugar and cream well together. Sift flour and baking powder and add alternately to the butter mixture. Have pans greased and floured and oven ready at moderate temperature, 375° F. At the very last moment fold in egg whites beaten stiff, and bake immediately.

FROSTING

2 cups sugar	2/3 cup water
	2 egg whites, beaten

Boil sugar and water without stirring until mixture spins a thread. Pour over whites and beat. Ice layers and top and sides of cake. Then sprinkle the grated fresh cocoanut over icing while still a little soft.

ANGEL FOOD CAKE

1 full cup egg whites	1 cup sifted cake flour
1 teaspoon cream tartar	¼ teaspoon salt
1½ cups granulated sugar	½ teaspoon almond flavoring
	½ teaspoon vanilla

Beat egg whites slightly, add cream of tartar, and continue beating until whites are stiff. Sift flour, sugar, and salt together four times. Slowly fold this into egg whites and add flavoring. Bake one hour in a slow oven.

CHOCOLATE ANGEL FOOD CAKE

1½ cups egg whites	2/3 cup cake flour
¼ teaspoon salt	1/3 cup cocoa
1½ cups sugar	1 teaspoon cream of tartar
½ teaspoon vanilla	

Beat egg whites with salt until stiff. Fold in sifted sugar very gradually. Sift flour once before measuring, then sift again with cocoa and cream of tartar. Fold into whites and sugar gradually. Add vanilla. Bake in ungreased angel cake pan. Put in cold oven, or very slow one, and gradually heat to about 350° F. Bake 45 minutes.

DELICIOUS SPONGE CAKE

Boil 1½ cups sugar and ½ cup water until syrup spins a thread. Separate 6 eggs and beat whites stiff. Add syrup slowly. Beat vigorously until the mixture is quite cool. Add beaten yolks, still beating briskly. Add 1 teaspoon vanilla. Fold in slowly 1 cup fine cake flour, which has been sifted before measuring. Add 1 pinch of salt and ¾ teaspoon cream of tartar. Then sift four times and add to mixture. Bake in slow oven, 325° F. about 1 hour in ungreased tubular pan.

SPONGE CAKE

5 eggs	½ teaspoon baking powder
1 cup sugar	¼ teaspoon salt
1 cup flour	1 teaspoon vanilla flavoring

Beat the yolks of eggs and sugar together. Add the

flour, baking powder, and salt, sifted together. Then cut in the whites beaten until very stiff. Add vanilla. Put in a deep cake tin and bake in a slow oven, 320° F. about forty minutes. Let cool in pan before taking it out.

THREE EGG SPONGE CAKE

3 eggs   1 cup sugar
1/3 cup of boiling water

Beat separately 3 egg whites, then 3 egg yolks. Add 1 cup sugar slowly to the beaten yolks. Then slowly add 1/3 cup of boiling water. Measure 1 cup of flour before it is sifted and sift and add to yolk mixture. If when flour is added, the batter seems too stiff to be beaten with a Dover egg beater, add a little more water. Add a pinch of salt and fold in the egg whites. Cook in small greased muffin or cup cake tins.

Oven: 325° F. Bake almost 30 minutes.

These are good dipped while hot in grated orange peel and orange juice frosting.

BLACK FRUIT CAKE

2 pounds raisins   1 pound butter
2 pounds currants, or 4   1 pound flour
  pounds raisins if preferred   1 dozen eggs
1 pound citron   1 tablespoon mace
1 pound almonds   1 tablespoon cinnamon
1 pound sugar   2 nutmegs

Cut up citron. Beat eggs light, and mix butter and sugar after they have been creamed together. Roll all fruit in flour and mix. Let rest of flour be lightly stirred in last.

AN ENGLISH RECIPE FOR DARK
FRUIT CAKE

1 pound shortening
1 pound pastry flour
1 tablespoon each, cinnamon, nutmeg, allspice
1 cup strawberry jam
1 box each, figs and dates
¾ pound each, crystallized cherries and pineapple

¼ pound each, orange and lemon peel
¼ pound each, pecans and walnuts
1 pound brown sugar
10 eggs
1 teaspoon soda
3 pounds raisins

½ pound citron

Cream the shortening and sugar and add the beaten yolks gradually. Add the jam. Use a little of the flour to dredge the fruit. Sift soda, cinnamon, nutmeg and allspice with remaining flour and add alternately with beaten egg whites. Add the fruit and nuts. Bake in deep well-greased pan in a slow oven, 250° F. about three hours.

CHRISTMAS PLUM CAKE

For a large plum cake allow:

1 pound, or a quart, of sifted flour
1 pound fresh butter cut up in a pound of powdered loaf sugar, in a deep pan
12 eggs
2 pounds raisins
2 pounds Zante currants
½ pound citron, either cut into slips or chopped fine

1 tablespoon of powdered mace and cinnamon, mixed
2 nutmegs, grated
1 large wine glass of Madeira, and
1 wine glass of French brandy mixed together and the spice steeped in it

Stir the butter and sugar to a light cream and add to

them the spice and liquor. Then beat the eggs in a shallow pan until very thick and smooth, breaking them one at a time into a saucer to ascertain if there is a bad one among them. One stale egg will spoil the whole cake. When the eggs are very light, stir them gradually into the large pan of butter and sugar in turn with the flour, that being the mixing pan. Lastly, add the fruit and citron, a little at a time of each, and give the whole a hard stirring. If the fruit is well-floured it will not sink, but it will be evenly dispersed all over the cake when baked.

Take a large straight sided block tin pan, grease it inside with the same butter used for the cake and put the mixture carefully in it. Set it immediately into a well-heated oven and keep up a steady heat while baking. When nearly done the cake will shrink a little from the sides of the pan. If it cracks on the top, it is proof of its being very light. When quite done, take it out. It will become hard if left to grow cold with the oven.

"SALLY WHITE" CAKE

WHITE FRUIT CAKE

1 pound butter
1¼ pounds sugar
1 pound flour
12 eggs
2 cocoanuts, grated
3 pounds citron, chopped

1 pound shelled almonds cut in small pieces
1 nutmeg
1 teaspoon cinnamon
1 teaspoon mace
1 wine-glass brandy or wine

Cream butter and gradually add the sugar. Beat eggs separate. Add yolks of eggs to sugar and butter. Add whites well-beaten. Then add brandy. Mix flour with fruit and add last.

PECAN CAKE

This cake is much liked by men, and is a cross between a pound cake and a fruit cake. It should be "aged" several weeks with brandy dripped over it after it is baked.

1 pound of flour	6 eggs, beaten separately
½ pound of butter	2 nutmegs, grated
1 pound of white sugar	1½ pounds seeded raisins
1 cup of brown sugar	1½ pounds shelled pecans
½ teaspoon of salt	½ pint sherry wine
1 teaspoon baking powder	½ pint brandy

Soak raisins in warm water and cut in pieces. Cut nuts in half and flour with some of flour. Mix cake as you would a pound cake, adding the nuts and raisins after everything is mixed, *except* the egg whites. Mix well. Lastly, add the stiffly beaten whites and *fold* in.

Cook as a fruit cake in lined, greased stem mold pan 3 or 4 hours in a very slow oven. If smaller pans are used, bake less time.

CANADIAN ORANGE CAKE

2 cups brown sugar	1 teaspoon soda, sifted twice
½ cup butter	¾ cup sour cream
2 eggs	1 cup raisins
2 cups flour	Grated rind of 1 orange

Bake in greased tube pan at 375° F. for 45 minutes to 1 hour. When the cake is taken from the oven, remove from pan and turn top side down. Over the bottom of the cake, pour the juice of 1 orange. This cake is better when a day old and will keep a long time. It is nice to have on hand for tea.

"Old Keswick"

MISS TAB HUYETT'S ORANGE CAKES

Prepare any good yellow batter cup cake recipe and bake according to directions.

Frosting or bath:

Juice of 2 oranges, more if
   not very juicy
Juice of 2 lemons

1¼ cups sugar
Grated rind of the oranges
   and lemons

Stir sugar so it won't lump or settle at the bottom. While cakes are hot, one at a time dip them in the juice mixture. This makes 6 dozen cakes.

MRS. BOURKE'S LITTLE SPICE CAKES

½ cup butter
1¼ cups brown sugar
½ cup milk
1½ cups flour
2 eggs beaten separately,
   whites from yolks

1½ teaspoons baking powder
1 teaspoon vanilla
1 tablespoon cinnamon
1 teaspoon cloves
1 teaspoon allspice
1 cup raisins

Cream butter and sugar. Add the beaten yolks of eggs, and milk. Then add flour, cinnamon, allspice, cloves, raisins floured lightly after washing off, vanilla, and baking powder. Lastly, add whites of egg, beaten very stiff, and bake.

This makes either little cakes or one large cake baked in pan with hole in center. Add two tablespoons of wine for large cake, and use any good white icing.

"Old Keswick"

SOFT CHOCOLATE FROSTING

Cut 4 squares bitter chocolate into small pieces and put into a saucepan. Add 1 cup sugar and 1½ cups milk.

Bring to the boiling point, stirring constantly. Mix 3 tablespoons cornstarch with 2 tablespoons cold water and add slowly to the first mixture, stirring until thickened. Remove from fire. Add 2 tablespoons butter and 1 teaspoon vanilla. Cool and spread.

ORANGE ICING

1 package confectioner's sugar	Grated rind of 1 orange and 1 lemon
About 3 tablespoons butter	Juice of 1 orange and 1 lemon

Put sugar in flat dish. Add a little fruit juice and rind, and softened butter. Then add rest of juice until of right consistency to spread on cake without being sticky.

STRAWBERRY ICING

Substitute strawberry juice, and proceed as for orange frosting.

MOCHA FILLING

1 cup butter	2 tablespoons coffee essence
2 cups powdered sugar	(Cook down left-over cof-
Yolks of 3 eggs	fee to make essence)

Cream butter and sugar together. Add three yolks of eggs, one at a time, and beat well. Flavor with the coffee essence, spread on cake and cover with whipped cream.

MOCHA ICING

1/3 cup butter	½ cup cocoa
2 cups powdered sugar	2 tablespoons strong coffee

Cream butter with sugar and cocoa until well-blended. Stir in coffee and beat until light and fluffy.

"Meadow Creek Farm"

CARAMEL FILLING

2 cups sugar   ½ cup water
Whites of 2 eggs

Put sugar and water into frying pan and cook until it becomes caramel. Beat the whites of the eggs to a stiff froth and pour the caramel into the eggs while it is hot. Beat the mixture until it is cold. This mixture will keep for several days.

LEMON FILLING

¼ cup butter   Grated rind of 1 lemon
1 cup sugar   6 tablespoons lemon juice,
3 eggs, slightly beaten   about 1½ lemons
⅛ teaspoon salt

Place butter in pan over hot water to soften. Add remaining ingredients. Cook over simmering water, stirring constantly until of good piling quality, about 15 minutes. Cool. Spread between layers of cake.

MISS BERTA'S ORANGE AND COCOANUT FROSTING

For Three or Four Layer Plain "1-2-3-4" Cake

Make usual boiled frosting with syrup over egg whites, using milk of fresh cocoanut in place of some of water in your recipe.

Have ready fresh grated cocoanut and whole orange sections with membrane removed. Three or four oranges will be needed. Spread bottom layer with frosting. Lay orange sections over, sprinkle with cocoanut, pressing all into frosting to stick. Repeat for second and third layers.

Ice top and sides and sprinkle with remaining cocoanut. Let stand at least six hours. On second and third days it is even better, though very sticky, as the orange and cocoanut have fermented slightly and soaked into the cake.

COCOANUT FROSTING

Thin 1 package of confectioner's sugar with cream. Add 3 tablespoons butter and mix until smooth. Add cocoanut.

Cookies

BENNE OR SESAME SEED CAKES

1 cup white sugar	1 teaspoon salt
¾ cup butter	1 teaspoon soda
3 slightly beaten eggs	2 cups flour
¼ cup brandy	1 cup lightly toasted, warm
2 cups flour	Benne seeds

Cream sugar and butter well, and eggs, sift in dry ingredients. Chill. Roll out very thin and sprinkle with a generous layer of warm, lightly-toasted Benne seeds, roll lightly over them to press in the cake. Cut with small fancy cutters and bake on an ungreased baking sheet at 350° F. until light golden brown.

Adapted by: *Mrs. Helen Duprey Bullock*
From: *"The Virginia Housewife"*
by Mrs. Mary Randolph
Second Edition—1825

"Seed cakes made from all the culinary seeds like carraway, coriander and cumin were great favorites in Virginia in the eighteenth or nineteenth century, but a selection of seed cakes made with Benne seeds is most appropriate as a choice for a Monticello Cook Book because Jefferson was very enthusiastic in cultivating them, and in trying to spread their culture in this country. He was interested in Benne oil as a delicate salad oil which could be substituted for olive oils imported from Europe."

MRS. CHALFIN'S SESAME COOKIES

1 cup flour	10 tablespoons white sugar
1 egg, well beaten	6 tablespoons brown sugar
½ cup shortening	1 teaspoon baking powder
½ teaspoon salt	4 tablespoons cocoanut
1 teaspoon almond flavoring	1 tablespoon milk

½ teaspoon sesame seed

Toast sesame seeds in oven with a little butter until slightly brown. Cream shortening and sugars. Add flavoring' and egg. Sift dry ingredients and add with milk. Mix in cocoanut and sesame seeds. Drop from spoon on greased cookie sheet and bake at 375° F. for about ten minutes.

SHREWSBURY CAKES

1 cup sugar	1 cup butter and Crisco, mixed
4 cups flour	
1 tablespoon cinnamon and nutmeg, mixed	3 eggs
	1½ teaspoons baking powder

Mix all dry ingredients and sift. Add eggs slightly beaten, butter and Crisco, and then baking powder. Knead this as well as you would for bread, until it is thoroughly mixed and easy to handle. Roll quite thin on floured board. Cut into shapes and bake in hot oven. This amount makes about five dozen average sized cookies.

WALNUT WAFERS

2 eggs	4 level tablespoons flour
1 cup walnuts	½ teaspoon Rumford baking powder
1 cup brown sugar	

¼ teaspoon salt

Beat eggs lightly, chop walnuts. Drop mixture from

small spoon on buttered pans, and bake about 10 or 12 minutes.

BLACK WALNUT COOKIES

Melt 1 pound of butter	1 teaspoon nutmeg
Add 2 cups brown sugar	1½ cups walnut meats,
1 egg	chopped fine
1 teaspoon cinnamon	Enough flour to handle

Mix and roll in two long rolls. Cover with oiled paper. Put in refrigerator at least 24 hours. Slice very thin. Cook 5-10 minutes in 400° F. oven. Remove cookies from pan with cake turner before they get cold. Lay on flat surface. They should be thin and brittle.

CHRISTMAS NUT CAKES

One pound pulverized sugar, one pound meats of hickory nuts, and whites of six eggs. Beat eggs for half an hour, then add sugar and nuts last. Bake on buttered papers in slow oven.

AN ENGLISH RECIPE FOR HAZEL NUT CREAMS

2 egg whites	1 teaspoon very strong coffee
½ cup fine granulated sugar	essence
¼ pound hazel nuts	

Grind nuts and add sugar. Beat egg whites stiff but *not* dry, and fold in nut mixture. Add coffee essence. Bake in moderate oven 15-20 minutes on sugared, buttered, pan. When cool, they look a little like macaroons. Then stick them together by twos with the following cream filling:

2 ounces butter	2 ounces powdered sugar
Flavor with coffee essence	

PECAN COOKIES

1 cup butter	2 cups chopped pecans
½ cup sugar	1 teaspoon vanilla
2 cups flour	1 tablespoon water

Mix with hand all ingredients until they stick together. Form dough in roll, wrap in waxed paper, making it airtight, put in icebox. This should chill enough to slice in an hour's time, but may be stored longer if well wrapped. Slice very thin and bake in a slow oven until cookies just begin to turn golden brown. Dust with confectioner's sugar while warm. Makes about 60 cookies.

SWEDISH ICE BOX NUT COOKIES

Cream together ¼ cup boiling water, 1 cup brown sugar, 1 cup white sugar, and 1 cup butter. Add ¼ teaspoonful cinnamon and beaten yolks of 2 eggs. Sift together 3½ cups flour, 1 teaspoonful salt, 1 teaspoonful baking powder, and ¼ teaspoonful soda. Add 1 cup nut meats, black walnuts, pecans or any nut meats. Beat egg whites and add to first mixture. Lightly fold in the flour. Roll into shape of sausage, wrap in oil paper, and let stand in ice-box overnight. Slice thin and bake on cookie sheet in moderate oven 10-12 minutes.

OATMEAL COOKIES

½ cup melted butter	1 egg
1 cup uncooked oatmeal	2 tablespoons flour
1 cup sugar	Pinch of salt
Vanilla	Pinch of baking powder

Mix together to a stiff paste. Roll in balls the size of a marble. Flatten out in greased, floured pan, not too close together as they spread somewhat. If desired, press in nut meats or ½ maraschino cherry. Cook in slow oven to moderate brown. Remove from pan immediately with cake lifter. This makes 2-3 dozen cookies.

"Dunlora"

LACE COOKIES

1 cup melted butter	2 cups uncooked oatmeal
3 cups brown sugar	1 cup pecans, chopped
1 egg	1 teaspoon vanilla

Cream butter and sugar, add beaten egg and vanilla, then mix in pecans and oatmeal. Drop mixture in pan by teaspoonful. Do not put too close together. Bake in moderate oven and let stay in pan a short time before removing.

DATE DIPS

6 tablespoons butter	1 teaspoon baking powder
1/3 cup sugar	½ teaspoon salt
1 egg	¼ cup heavy cream
1 cup flour	½ teaspoon vanilla

3 cups dates, pitted

Put a nut in each date. Cream butter, sugar, and cream. Add egg and beat. Mix and sift flour, baking powder, salt, and add to first mixture. Add vanilla.

Dip dates, one by one, in batter and place on a buttered cookie sheet. Bake in a moderate hot oven, 375° F. for about 10-12 minutes.

MRS. DOREMUS' RUM CAKES

3 ten cent packages of vanilla wafers	3 tablespoons white Karo
	Pinch salt
3 jiggers of rum	½ cup pecans

Crumble the wafers to crumbs, mix other ingredients, and form with hands into balls or patties and roll in powdered sugar. Let harden.

ROLLED COOKIES

1 beaten egg	1 heaping teaspoon butter
1 cup brown sugar, lightly packed	½ teaspoon salt
	1 teaspoon vanilla
2 tablespoons flour	1 cup finely ground pecans

Mix all ingredients and drop from teaspoon on well buttered pan. Mash flat with potato masher that has been dipped in cold water and shaken dry. Bake at 350° F. until lightly brown. Work fast and roll over handle of wooden spoon. If too hard to roll, run back in oven to soften them.

BUTTER FINGERS

½ pound butter	3 cups sifted flour
3 heaping tablespoons sugar	Vanilla
Pinch of salt	1 cup pecans

Work butter into flour, to which sugar and salt have been added, as for pastry. Add vanilla and crumbled nuts.

Form into small oblong pieces about the shape and size of the thumb. Bake at 350° F. until *lightly* brown and roll in powdered sugar while hot.

Candies

A NEW ORLEANS RECIPE FOR NOUGAT

Two cups pecans, chopped fine, using a baking powder can to chop with, and 1½ cups white sugar, or 1¼ cups, if weather is cold.

Melt sugar, as for caramel, add pecans and let cool for about two minutes. Butter a biscuit board, then dampen it thoroughly. Pour candy on this and roll to required thickness with rolling pin that has been rubbed with butter and dampened. Cut into squares at once. Most prefer about three-eighths inch in thickness. Do not use a marble slab for this candy, as it cools too quickly on this.

BLACK WALNUT CANDY

2 cups white Karo	⅛ teaspoon salt
½ cup butter	2 cups white sugar
1 large can evaporated milk	1 teaspoon vanilla

1 cup chopped walnuts

Cook at 245° F., add flavoring and nuts, stir constantly while cooking. Pour into buttered pan. Let cool 3 hours. Cut like caramel.

"Upper Pantops"

COCOANUT CANDY

2 pounds sugar	2 tablespoons vinegar
1 cocoanut	1 cup water

Boil sugar, water, vinegar until it forms a soft ball in cold water. Add grated cocoanut and boil again until just stiff enough to pick up in fingers from cold water. Set aside to cool, when lukewarm, beat well and as it gets creamy, drop from end of spoon onto greased dishes making small "pralines".

CHOCOLATE NUT FUDGE

2 cups sugar	½ teaspoon salt
1½ cups corn syrup	3 tablespoons butter
1½ cups cream or milk	1 teaspoon vanilla

1½ cups roasted almonds

Cook sugar, syrup, and cream to a hard ball, stirring all the time. Add butter and cook back to hard ball. Take from fire, add vanilla, nuts and pour into a flat greased pan until cool. Pour over this one-quarter pound melted bitter chocolate and sprinkle ground almonds on top.

PEANUT BRITTLE

1 pound roasted peanuts	3 cups granulated sugar

1 teaspoon soda

Shell peanuts, roll slightly with rolling pin, and add soda. Put sugar in frying pan and heat slowly until it is a smooth brown syrup, stirring constantly. Add peanuts and soda. Mix thoroughly. Put on a buttered tin. Mark while hot for cutting with knife. Proportion of soda and peanuts may be varied.

NEW ORLEANS PRALINES

1 pound brown sugar	Little water
½ pound shelled pecans	Pinch of baking soda

Moisten sugar with water, let boil, stirring frequently.

When it forms a firm ball in cold water, stir in small pinch of soda. Stir hard until it begins to feel sugary around edges of pot. Then add pecans, take from fire and continue to stir until it becomes creamy, soft creamy.

Drop from spoon onto saucers, which have been buttered well. When slightly cool, slip from saucers with fingers. This makes the flat praline, as sold in New Orleans. If more nuts are desired, they can be used so as to make the mounded praline.

Note: For Benne Pralines use the regular recipe for pralines but substitute 2 tablespoons sesame seeds for the pecan meats.

GLACED FRUITS

¾ cup boiling water   2 cups sugar

Boil rapidly until syrup begins to turn brown. Add a little vanilla, put fruit or nuts into the syrup, and take out with fork and drop on marble slab. The following can be used: dates, cherries, nuts and white grapes with the stems left on.

SPICED NUTS

1 cup nuts	½ teaspoon cinnamon
1 egg white	¼ tablespoon cloves or nut-
4 tablespoons confectioner's	meg
sugar	⅛ teaspoon salt

Beat egg white. Add sugar, spice, and salt. Add nuts and when well-covered, spread in a thin layer on buttered pan. Bake 30 minutes in a very slow oven.

STUFFED FIGS

Pulled figs	Raisins
Walnut kernels	Granulated sugar
Marshmallows	Liquor

Soak figs overnight in any kind of liquor, brandy preferably. Make a hole at the round end with a small sharp knife. Put in half walnut kernels, one-half marshmallow, three or four raisins, roll in sugar. Let the stem stand up.

Preserves and Pickles

STRAWBERRY PRESERVES

One quart of strawberries, one quart of sugar, put into a saucepan, let come to boil, then add another quart of berries and another quart of sugar. Let all boil together hard for 20 minutes, stirring all the time, then it is all ready to be put into the hot glass jars that have been sitting in water. This will keep for years and is very delicious.

"Cloverfields"

STRAWBERRY PRESERVES

Allow one and one-half cups sugar to each cup of strawberries. Let stand, without stirring, until sugar is dissolved. Cook twenty minutes. These preserves will be a deep, rich red, and the berries large and clear.

"Fairview Farm"

Note: Let strawberry preserves cool in shallow pan overnight, then pour into sterile jars and seal. This distributes fruit throughout syrup.

GRAPE CONSERVE

Seed grapes, and put in skins and pulp until there are 4 full cups. Add 7 cups of sugar, 3 oranges sliced very thin, 1 cup of seedless raisins, and bring to a boil. Boil 5 minutes. Add 1 bottle of Certo. Put 1 cup of English walnut meats, uncooked, and evenly distributed, into bottom of jelly glasses. Pour hot ingredients into glasses on top of the nuts. Seal with paraffin while still hot, and reseal when cold.

If a good many of the grapes are unripe, the flavor will be better, more tangy.

This recipe made with white grapes is unusually good.

PLUM CONSERVE

6 pounds plums   4 oranges, pulp and grated
6 pounds sugar   rind
2 pounds raisins

Cook to the consistency of marmalade and when partly cold, add one pound of broken English walnuts.

Note: Green gage plums are especially good in this recipe.

RASPBERRY JAM

Allow equal parts of sugar and berries. Mash berries and cook in their own juice for one-half hour, stir often, then add one-quarter of the sugar and boil five minutes. Then add more sugar, boil again and so on, until sugar is all used.

ORANGE MARMALADE

4 oranges, sliced thin   3 pints water
2 lemons, sliced thin   2¾ pounds sugar

Let stand twenty-four hours. Boil one-half hour. Add sugar and boil one-half hour. Let stand twenty-four hours. Boil one-half hour and pour into jelly glasses.

BRANDIED PEACHES

6 pounds ripe peaches	3 pounds white sugar
Brandy	2 cups water

Pare the peaches with knife, never scalding and skinning them as is usual for canning. Drop into boiling sugar syrup and cook until just tender, about 5 minutes. Put into hot jars, cover one-half to three-quarters full with hot syrup, fill remainder with good brandy. Cover. Let stand overnight and if shrunk in the morning, add more brandy to fill, cap tightly, and put away in a cool place. The best brandied peaches are those made with the best and most brandy.

BRANDIED PEACHES

Use cling stones, ripening late.

Pare peaches and put in fruit jar. Fill the jar with white granulated sugar. Shake and strike jar with palm of hand until sugar has sifted down and filled all the spaces. Screw top on jar and put away in dark cellar. Next day force another peach into the jar, fill again with sugar, screw top on over the rubber, tight as possible. Wrap jar in paper and put away in dark place, where temperature will not be under forty or over seventy-five. The longer they are allowed to stand the better.

"Midmont"

SPICED PEACHES

7 pounds peaches	2 ounces root-ginger, ground
4 pounds sugar	2 teaspoons mace
1 pint vinegar	2 teaspoons cinnamon
	2 teaspoons allspice

Pare peaches, but do not remove stones. Make small

squares of muslin to hold spices. Put all in kettle and bring to a boil. Pour into stone crock. Next day pour off juice and bring to a boil, pouring over fruit and spices. Do this nine days. On ninth day, boil down syrup to right consistency. Then put in fruit and let all come to a boil. Put in glass jars and seal while hot.

GINGER PEARS

Peel and cut into small pieces, 10 pounds pears. Add 7 pounds sugar. Cook slowly for one hour. Add 4 lemons, 6 oranges, and 1 pound crystallized ginger, cut into small pieces.

Let all simmer for 3 hours. Put in hot sterilized jars.

ARTICHOKE PICKLE

½ peck artichokes	3½ cups sugar
4 large onions	3 pints vinegar
2 tablespoons mustard seed	2 tablespoons white celery
1 teaspoon salt	seed

Scrape and grind Jerusalem artichokes and onions in meat chopper, very coarse. Mix well the ingredients and simmer for 30 minutes. Pack in jars and wait a few days before using.

"Flordon"

DAMSON PICKLE

Ten pounds of fruit, six pounds of sugar, one quart of vinegar, one tablespoon each of whole cloves, allspice and cinnamon. Wash the damsons and put in a jar. Scald the vinegar, sugar and spices and pour over the damsons. Repeat this for five mornings, and on the fifth, boil all together for half an hour.

"Credenhill"

CHILI SAUCE

30 ripe tomatoes	4 cups brown sugar
12 onions	1 quart cider vinegar
6 pears	3 tablespoons salt
6 peaches	½ tablespoon cloves
3 red peppers	1 tablespoon cinnamon
3 sweet green peppers	1 tablespoon allspice

1 tablespoon celery seed

Put all through a grinder. Cook slowly two and one-half hours. Bottle and seal.

FRENCH RELISH

12 green peppers	2 bunches celery
12 red peppers	4 cups white sugar
1 quart onions	3 tablespoons mustard seed
1 quart vinegar	3 tablespoons celery seed

3 scant teaspoons salt

Cut celery and peppers in blocks about one-half inch. Grind onions through meat chopper. Cover all with boiling water and let stand five minutes. Drain and cover again with boiling water and let stand ten miuntes. Drain, add vinegar, sugar, seasoning. Let boil for fifteen minutes and cover in glass jars while hot.

"Dunlora"

PLANTATION GARDENS' PEPPER PICKLE
WITH HERBS

12 large green peppers
12 sweet red peppers
4 small onions
3 tablespoons thyme leaves
5 tablespoons chives
2 stalks celery or smallage (wild cherry)
1 sprig French tarragon

2 sprigs summer savory
1 teaspoon of one of the lemon flavored herbs, lemon verbena or balm or lemon basil
1 pint boiling water
3 cups white vinegar
2 cups sugar

2 tablespoons salt

Remove seeds from peppers and chop in food grinder. Pour the hot water over them and let stand for ten minutes. Drain well and add chopped onions, vinegar, sugar and salt. Boil for twenty minutes, then add the fresh green herbs. These should be finely chopped, and simmer one minute. Seal immediately.

The total quantity of chopped herbs is about three-quarters of a cupful. This recipe makes seven half-pint jars.

SWEET CUCUMBER PICKLES

Take good sized cucumbers and put in a brine that will float an egg. They can be used after being in the brine for two weeks, but they are just as good after being in brine for six months or a year. Slice a quarter of an inch thick and soak twenty-four hours in fresh water, changing water several times. Boil in strong alum water one-half hour, then boil in strong ginger tea thirty minutes. Make a syrup of three pounds of white sugar, one quart of vinegar, one pint of water, some cinnamon, cloves and a little mace. Put in the cucumbers and boil until clear and the syrup is thick. If this is not sufficient to cover, make a little more.

"Credenhill"

GREEN TOMATO PICKLE

1 peck of green tomatoes	1 teaspoon of turmeric
2 quarts of onion	½ pound white mustard seed
1 gallon vinegar	½ ounce ground mace
2 pounds brown sugar	1 tablespoon celery seed
½ tablespoon of cayenne	1 tablespoon ground cloves
¼ tablespoon ground mustard	

Slice the tomatoes and onion very thin, sprinkle a little salt through them and let them stand overnight. Drain them through a colander and put them on to boil with enough vinegar to cover them and boil slowly until they are clear and tender. Then drain them from the vinegar. Put into some fresh vinegar the sugar, mustard seed, mace, celery seed, and cloves, and let them boil for a few minutes, then pour it over the drained tomatoes which have been mixed with the cayenne pepper, ground mustard and turmeric. Mix them well together. When cold, put into jars.

SLICED TOMATO PICKLE

½ bushel green tomatoes	2 teaspoons cinnamon
1 quart onions	2 teaspoons cloves
6 green peppers	2 teaspoons allspice
2 handsful horseradish	2 teaspoons black pepper
4 pounds brown sugar	½ pound white mustard seed
4 tablespoons mustard	¼ pound celery seed
2 tablespoons ginger	¼ pound turmeric

1 nutmeg

Slice tomatoes, onion and pepper the night before.

Sprinkle with a cup of salt and drain overnight in cotton bag. Add spices, sugar, and so forth. Cover with good vinegar and cook until clear.

"Dunlora"

CHOPPED TOMATO PICKLE

1 peck green tomatoes	1 dozen red peppers
1 dozen green peppers	1 dozen large onions

Cut all, add one-half cup salt and let stand overnight. Drain and add vinegar to cover and three pounds of sugar. Boil one hour. Just before taking up, add:

4 tablespoons celery seed	2 teaspoons ground mace
4 ounces mustard	½ cup scraped horseradish
2 teaspoons ground cloves	

Seal in jars while hot.

CHOW-CHOW PICKLE

½ peck green tomatoes	2 large heads cabbage
15 large white onions	25 cucumbers

Cut these up, pack in salt for a night, drain and then soak in vinegar and water for two days. Then drain again. Mix with the following:

1 pint grated horseradish	½ cup cinnamon
½ pound white mustard seed	½ pint small white onions
½ cup ground black pepper	1 ounce celery seed
½ cup turmeric	

Cover with 1½ gallons boiling hot vinegar, boil until tender, mixing in it 2 boxes mustard, 3 pounds brown sugar, and ½ pint good olive oil.

WATERMELON PICKLE

Soak medium-sized watermelon rind with one ounce of Lily's lime in enough water to cover. Pour off in morning, wash in cold water and boil three times, ten minutes each time, in fresh water. Make syrup as follows: one cup of vinegar to two cups of sugar. Make enough syrup to cover rinds well. Season with cloves, cinnamon, and mace to taste, tied in a muslin bag. Use cinnamon lightly. Cook slowly until clear.

WATERMELON RIND PICKLE

Boil 10 pounds watermelon rind, peeled and sliced into small squares in enough water to cover it. Put ½ cup of salt in water, boil ½ hour. Take out rind and soak in clear water 15 minutes.

Drain rind, put in a kettle and cover with vinegar. Take out rind and measure vinegar. To every quart of vinegar, add 3 pounds of sugar and one tablespoon each of cinnamon, cloves and allspice. Let boil up, add rind and boil 15 minutes. Take out rind and put in jars. Add 2 pounds more of sugar to each quart of vinegar, boil ½ hour longer until thick, pour over rind and seal. Remove spices from vinegar after the first boiling. About 1½ quarts of vinegar is enough.

Put spices in a muslin bag. If vinegar is very strong, substitute 1 cup of water and give light weight on sugar.

This makes about 5 quarts.

"Union Hall"

YELLOW CABBAGE PICKLE

Select cabbages not too large, quarter and sprinkle with salt. Let stand overnight, wash out salt and cook until tender in weak vinegar into which enough turmeric is added to color, yellow. Throw this vinegar away and to one-half gallon of fresh vinegar, put a scant pound of brown sugar, one tablespoon of ground mustard, mixed smooth, one small teaspoon of whole cloves, whole all-spice, whole black pepper, a few sticks of cinnamon, a little mace and root ginger. Boil for five minutes. Place cabbages in a jar, sprinkle celery seed and white mustard seed between the layers. Pour hot vinegar over and add a few cloves of one or two medium-sized onions. When cold, tie up and keep in cool, dry place.

"Credenhill"

Cooking Hints

Heat butter and milk together and beat into mashed potatoes. This makes them light and airy.

A quick way to chop nuts is to place them in a dry cloth and roll with a rolling pin.

Cheese will never get mouldy if you rub the cut part with butter and cover with waxed paper.

Let potatoes stand fifteen minutes in hot water before baking and it will take half the time to bake them.

A pinch of brown sugar will overcome the salty taste in over-salted soup and will not be noticeable.

When the baby first starts having cereal, an after-dinner coffee spoon will be found much easier to use than a regular baby spoon.

If you do not have cake flour for your cake, use ordinary flour but sift it five times with one teaspoonful of cornstarch added.

A lump of sugar put in to boil with vegetables will preserve the color and improve the flavor, especially peas.

Rub a chicken inside with a lemon cut in halves before baking. This will make the meat white, juicy and tender.

Save bacon fat in jar on back of stove and use in frying and seasoning vegetables. This seems to be one of the earliest Virginia culinary customs. Suggestions for other uses: in cheese souffle, to grease baking dishes, for frying fish.

A ham bone should be used for flavoring when boiling navy beans, split peas, or "greens".

Before squeezing the juice from your lemons or oranges, grate the peel. Wrap in waxed paper and put in refrigerator to be handy for flavorings in desserts, puddings, and cakes.

Orange and lemon peel grated over a cake before the icing is put on will flavor the cake all through.

If a few drops of vinegar are added to the water in which eggs are to be poached, they will hold together and the white will not separate in the water.

Add the juice from pickled peaches or watermelon pickle to the liquid for baking ham.

QUANTITIES OF MATERIALS REQUIRED FOR ENTERTAINING 100 PERSONS

POTATO SALAD

For three and a half gallons use: One and a half pecks of potatoes, or twenty-one pounds, three large bunches celery, one pound of onions and three quarts mayonnaise; or, a dressing of yolks of thirty eggs, one and a half pounds of butter, one teacup of sugar, one half dozen lemons, one pint of vinegar.

CHICKEN SALAD

Eight large chickens, weighing about four pounds each, two large bunches of celery.

Dressing: Yolks of forty eggs, two pints of vinegar, eight lemons, teacupful of sugar, one-half pound of butter.

SANDWICHES

Six loaves of bread, two hundred small beaten biscuits.

COFFEE

Three gallons of coffee made of three pounds of coffee. One pint of coffee will pour five after-dinner cups.

CHOCOLATE

One and one-half gallons of chocolate made of two pounds of chocolate.

ALMONDS

Four pounds of salted almonds.

PICKLE

One-half gallon of small pickles.

BON-BONS

Eight pounds of mints.

ICE CREAM

Four gallons of ice cream.

MAYONNAISE

Seven quarts of olive oil, six eggs to each quart of oil, one pint of vinegar, one dozen lemons, red pepper.

Household Hints

"Method is the Soul of Management."

Mrs. Mary Randolph
"The Virginia Housewife"
Fourth Edition, Published 1830

HOUSEHOLD HINTS

Brass knockers and door knobs that are exposed to the weather will keep clean and bright longer if rubbed with paraffin or wax after they are polished.

Fresh ink stains can be removed from a rug if the mark is gently rubbed with a moist rag dipped in cream of tartar or French chalk. After this treatment, wash the spot with warm water.

Marks left by hot plates and dishes on a dining room table can usually be removed by applying spirits of camphor with a soft cloth. Rub lightly and when the stain disappears, polish with a soft duster.

Iodine stains will come out of almost any article if soaked in lime water.

Wash out discarded velours powder puffs and keep them for polishing silver, shoes, etc.

Dry mustard removes fish odor from one's hands and from pans.

Vinegar and salt will clean copper and brass very effectively. Use two tablespoons of salt to a cup of vinegar.

Before going to work in your garden, put soap under

your fingernails. This will be a great aid in keeping your hands in good condition.

Fruit stains on the fingers can easily be removed if rubbed with oatmeal moistened with vinegar or lemon juice, before applying soap.

Windows may be kept clean during the winter if rubbed occasionally with glycerin, then polished with a dry cloth.

To clean windows, put a tablespoon of vinegar with a tablespoon of ammonia in a gallon of water. Crumpled newspapers are good to use instead of rags.

Bread crumbs rubbed on scorched cloth will cause the brown to disappear.

A good homemade furniture polish consists of equal parts of vinegar, boiled linseed oil and pure gum turpentine. Shake well before using. Frequent use will not only clean and polish furniture but will, in time, give a mellow finish.

"To drive red ants away thickly sprinkle a mixture of powdered clove and allspice about where the ants are and allow to remain. The smell is very distasteful to them."

From The Bean Pot—Cape Cod

POT-POURRI

Gather rose petals every day before they have lost some of their sweetness, and partially dry them in the sun. Twenty-four hours is time enough to shrivel them a little. Before putting the rose leaves in the jar, it is well to put in 5 drops of oil of rose geranium mixed with the same amount of glycerine to prevent evaporation. Add the freshly dried leaves as they are secured, and with each lot that is put in the jar, add a teaspoonful of alcohol to retain the natural scent. When all the leaves that can be had are gathered and in the jar, sprinkle a little salt over them and shake every day for a couple of weeks until they are partly "ripened", then add ¼ ounce of allspice, ¼ ounce of nutmeg, ¼ ounce of cinnamon, 1 ounce of orris-root, 1 ounce of dried lavender flowers, and a few heliotrope if they can be had. A half-ounce of finely crushed tonquin-bean can also be added. Keep the jar covered except when it is wanted to perfume the room. Then add a few drops of alcohol to it, to enhance its fragrance and also to preserve the odor of the contents.